Third edition, revised 2012

First published in 2006 by
WOODFIELD PUBLISHING
Bognor Regis, West Sussex, England
www.woodfieldpublishing.com

ISBN 1-84683-018-4

A Member of the
Royal Air Force
'Of Indeterminate Race'

*Wartime Memoirs of a former
RAF Navigator & POW*

CY GRANT

Woodfield

In memory of all the young airmen who lost their lives in the last world war and particularly the Aircrew from the West Indies and West Africa, some of whom served with great distinction but whose memory is still unsung - the dark side of the story of the Few.

I would also like to dedicate this book to the members of my crew in recognition of the strong bond forged in the very short period spent together in training and on operations; as well as the eleven members of my prisoner of war mess, with whom I shared a single room for the best part of two years:

The most striking part of this chapter of my life story is that in the midst of the trauma and destruction of war, we find the making and resolution of a personal tragedy in Holland, the formation of a lasting bond between Canadian and West Indian and English and Dutch, forged in the skies over Germany, and a relevant and compelling comment on racial attitudes of the time and how it affected and continues to affect my entire life.

Contents

"Have you perhaps request for such a machine"
civilian - Pole - razor -

Procession of the Wounded.
I thought this lowest poss. form of existence, and
then I saw 5,000 Americans herded into
dank tents,
- a "goose" is stolen -
A worse plight? Bavarian Soldiers,
at Belaria They spoke of women.
Here it is "My Favourite Dish"
My Shirt for 20 cigarettes: issues
German mother's pity — milk
Haben sie brot für zigaretten?
Norweigians present you with ....
food to Self-Respect.
After 5 weeks of Starvation

4½ weeks of food - intermittent Sunshine t
good news,
April 9th Rumour of move to Moosburg,-
  " 11th 2 G.C. moved (Captured?)
  " 12th Leave Camp, Bad Cans - 40
  " 13th Picnic Luckenwalde
  " 14th Return Camp - no available
      Franfut Reception -
      POTSDAM RAIL,
  " 16th Soviets on the move again - Stettin - Frankfurt
      Niesse
change in German attitude.
Days of anxiety, bright sunshine, + air activity
      Rumours are rife
April 19th Flap at Mid-Night. Prepare to meet
      Reminons of Russian break through

Page from Author's notes made in captivity as a POW.

~ ii ~

Acknowledgements

I'd like to acknowledge my publishers, Woodfield Publishing, for making this memoir available to the general public, many of whom are unaware of the historic contribution made by West Indian and West African aircrew in World War 2; also the Imperial War Museum, London for housing these memoirs; the Ministry of Defence "We Were There" Touring Schools Exhibition for making the contribution of ethnic minorities in wartime better known; Flight Lieutenant Vernon White of the Canadian Air Force and a fellow prisoner of war, who read the manuscript whilst still in preparation; Walter Langille, the son of my Canadian pilot, Flight Lieutenant Alton Langille, for sending me his father's account of The March and our time at Lukenwalde, POW camp; David Fell of RAF Elsham Wolds Association (incorporating 103 Squadron), for providing photos and information about operations over Germany during 1943; Joost Klootwyk who after a long and arduous investigation successfully documented the details of the last flight of Lancaster W4901 on the fatal night when we were shot down over Haarlem in Holland; and the personal reminiscences of survivors of our crew; Ian Dieffenthaller for his editorial help and insightful suggestions regarding the inclusion of some of my POW poems; Roger Lambo for information about African aircrew and technical information about Lancaster Bombers;; Laurent (Laurie) Phillpotts of the West Indian Ex-Servicemen's Association for keeping the memory of Caribbean ex-servicemen alive; and last, but not least, Mia Morris of Wellplaced Consultancy for her support and encouragement.

During the last months of the war I kept a day-by-day diary of events (see page ii). I am also heavily indebted to the POW publication *The Log*, privately published by Squadron Leader Bryce Cousens in 1947, for material mostly corroborating my version of events and for additional official material relating to events in the last months of the war.

The Author, RAF Flight Lieutenant, 1945.

Preface

My war experiences as a Guyanese war veteran are today housed in the archives of the Imperial War Museum. This book is an attempt to put them into a wider framework and include a brief description of my early life in a British Colony and my reasons for joining up when for the first time non-whites from the British Commonwealth were allowed into the RAF.

This account is not about any heroics on my part, but rather to make readers aware that black people from the British Commonwealth served in the Royal Air Force during World War II, not only as aircrew but also as commissioned officers. My narrative is mainly about the time I spent incarcerated as a prisoner of war in Germany, having been shot down after only three operational flights during the Battle of the Ruhr in 1943.

Many stories of the involvement of black aircrew from the Caribbean and West Africa that still are not generally known – stories of bravery and outstanding gallantry that have been lost because this subject has not officially been researched and also possibly because of a reluctance to acknowledge the exploits of the invisible dark few who flew in World War II.

We now know that there were between 300 and 500 West Indian aircrew out of a total of around six thousand non-white volunteers who served in the Royal Air Force during the war. About 70 were commissioned and 103 received decorations. The names of a few distinguished West Indian aircrew are on record at the RAF Museum in London, but many still remain unacknowledged. I, personally, knew aircrew from both groups.

People like:

- Squadron Leader Ulric Cross, DSO DFM
- Warrant Officer Owen Sylvester DFM
- Flight Lieutenant Lawrence Osborne [became a Group Captain] and Flight Sergeant E.A. Joseph from Trinidad
- Wing Commander Powell
- Squadron Leader J.T. (Jimmy) Barrowes
- Flight Lieutenant Robert Rubie DFC
- Flight Leutenant John Ebanks DFC
- Flight Lieutenant John Blair DFC
- Flight Lieutenant Dudley Thompson
- Flight Lieutenant Arthur Wint
- Flight Lieutenant Ivor De Souza
- Flight Lieutenant Vincent Bunting
- Flight Lieutenant Billy Strachan
- Flight Lieutenant Dundas
- Flight Lieutenant David Chance
- Flight Lieutenant William Richardson
- Flight Sergeant John Burke
- Flight Sergeant Don Bourne
- Flight Lieutenant Huntley DaCosta
- Flying Officer Gilbert Fairwether
- Flying Officer John Bonitto
- Flying Officer Oliver Marshall

- Flying Officer H. Capstick
- Flight Engineer Tony Hill
- Flight Sergeant Vernon Lindo
- Flight Sergeant Ralph Chevannes
- Flight Sergeant Lloyd Wint
- Flight Sergeant Harry Shaw
- Flight Sergeant Peter Brown and Flight Sergeant Tucker, from Jamaica
- Flight Lieutenant Osmond Kelsick DFC from Monserrat
- Flight Lieutenant Edward (Scobie) Dalrymple from Dominica
- Warrant Officer John Rowan Henry, from Antigua
- Flight Lieutenant Ronald Hall and Flying Officer Cecil (Dusty) Miller from Guyana
- Flying Officer Errol Barrow
- Flight Lieutenant A.O. Weekes and Pilot Officer Ardel Inness from Barbados
- Flying Officer Julian Marryshaw from Grenada

Unfortunately, there are many others who remain unacknowledged, their names lost in the mists of time.

It should be noted that only about thirty percent of all aircrew in Bomber Command were commissioned as officers for the duration of the war, a pertinent fact considering that among the West Indian aircrew I have identified above, there was such a high proportion of officers. This contrasts with the official assumption, a few years earlier, about the suitability of black airmen to join the Royal Air Force, and for that matter, the assumptions, even today, about the ability of black people in all spheres of involvement in society.

There were also a number of West Africans who flew with the RAF, some of whom were commissioned. Flight Lieutenant Peter Adenyi Thomas (Nigeria) was the first, followed by Flight Lieutenant Johnny Smythe (Sierra Leone), and Pilot Officer Adesanya Hyde DFC (Ghana). Non commissioned officers included Flight Sergeant Bankole Vivour (Nigeria) and Flight Sergeant Akin Shenbanjo (Nigeria) whose Halifax bomber was christened *Achtung! The Black Prince!*[1] In all there were about fifty West Africans as aircrew.

It should also be noted that there were RAF aircrew from all over the British Commonwealth and beyond – Ceylon (Sri Lanka), India, Canada, Australia and New Zealand.[2]

But recognition of the contribution made by Africans and West Indians in the last war has been slow in coming. In 2000 the Ministry of Defence belatedly launched the exhibition *We were There* "to honour the invaluable contribution made by all ethnic minorities to the Armed Forces." Two years later, the Memorial Gates on Constitution Hill were inaugurated by Queen Elizabeth II. The Gates were erected as a "lasting memorial to honour the five million men and women from the Indian subcontinent, Africa and the Caribbean

---

[1] For further information see *Achtung! The Black Prince*, Roger Lambo in Africaans in Britain, ed. David Killingray, Frank Cass, 1994.
[2] See *Our War: How the British Commonwealth fought the Second World War* Christopher Somerville, Cassell Reference & *The British Empire & the Second World War*, Ashley Jackson, Hambledon.

who volunteered to serve with the Armed Forces during the First and Second World Wars."[3]

Whilst recognizing that our debt to black and other overseas service men has not been fully documented, I should like to make it quite clear that any revival of interest in the war is no cause for celebration. For me, warfare is but a fraction of mankind's evolving consciousness and my part of it, merely one incident in the microscopic continuum of my own evolving consciousness. Ideally, then, the war memoir should be read in the context of my experiences as a black person who has lived in Britain for over six decades: time enough to observe the inherently catastrophic construct of so-called Western materialist dialectics – the underpinning of, among other things, nationalism, racism and humanity's self-alienation from its natural sustaining environment. Unless we are informed by the past we will never know who we are, where we are going and what we can do to help shape the future history of us all.

Shortly after I was captured I was put into solitary confinement for one week, then dragged out to be photographed. The picture appeared in the German Newspaper *Volkischer Beobachter*, July 1943, with the caption "A

---

[3] About 350,000 Africans served in the British army in the Middle East, North Africa and East Africa, Europe and the Far East; of these 3,387 were killed. Another 500,000 Africans fought for the French. According to French authorities, some 39,000 of those were killed. Historian C.R. Gibbs writes:

"For the Allied powers, Africa was a reservoir of manpower, a storehouse of raw materials, a treasure chest of vital funds, and an important theatre of military operations" [*African Perspective*, April 2005].

member of the Royal Air Force of indeterminate race" Presumably this was meant as a propaganda exercise for Nazi Master Race doctrine, implying that the RAF had to resort to the recruitment of people of unknown or 'undeterminable' race to fight their wars for them. Indeed, from a limited perspective, there is an element of truth in this – for the simple reason that at the beginning of the war, the Royal Air Force did not countenance the recruitment of 'men of colour' into its distinguished ranks. To actually commission some as officers might have been seen to demonstrate just how degenerate the RAF had become.

The main point of this memoir, however, is an invitation to make an honest appraisal of the dilemma we all face. As a prisoner of war for two years, I had enough time to reflect on the unusual predicament in which I found myself – fighting a racist Nazi regime whilst being subject to racism in my own backyard; a situation albeit tempered during my days before capture, by the exigencies of the threat to Britain.

There has certainly been progress on the racial front in Britain. Today the RAF can even boast a Guyanese Air Commodore, David Case, and we are accustomed to seeing black and Asian presenters on tv, as trade union leaders, doctors in our hospitals and in tv soaps; Olympic champions draped in the Union Jack, footballers playing for England, even MPs, baronesses and Peers of the Realm. But what was it like in the 40s and 50s in Britain? I believe that my experiences are typical of those of black people at that time, and about attitudes that are still with us today.

In my case, after the war I qualified as a barrister at law but unable to enter Chambers, or to find a job anywhere, I was forced to find employment in show business. I played many roles as an actor and singer in order to survive, the classic example being cast in the late fifties as a calypso singer on BBC TV's *Tonight* programme, thus becoming the first black face to appear regularly on British Television. This was to lead to my part in Gerry Anderson's successful sci-fi series, *Captain Scarlet*, voicing the puppet character Lieutenant Green, purportedly based on me! Given that I'd been a real life navigator of a Lancaster Bomber during World War II, this might have been a more valid reason, had it been known, for basing the character on me, but Gerry should be credited for creating the first black character to appear in a highly successful sci-fi series.

That the contribution made by black servicemen is only now slowly being acknowledged is due to the unspoken racism that still bedevils our misconceptions about 'race'. What do we mean by race? There is only one human race. We not only have to acknowledge the contribution of the dark few, but work together to achieve a decent society for all.

The Author, RAF Leading Aircraftman, 1941.

Foreword

What I dream today... I can realise tomorrow. A dream job and ability honed in Britain. I am actually quite proud of the fact that my Britishness has a unique place in the world. Many fought and died to give me the chance to be who I wanted to be. I started working in media in 1981. I then joined the BBC two years later and it has been a roller coaster ride that has taken me all over the world. I have won awards and had many firsts.

Over the years as a TV producer and radio broadcaster, I have had the pleasure of meeting and working with some the most influential names in the history of politics, science, sport and entertainment. Many of the names from Nelson Mandela, Jeremy Clarkson to Quincy Jones, to the many stars of the Motown record label such as Stevie Wonder and the Jacksons, and UK icons Freddie Mercury and Queen, all formed a part of my youthful admiration. What a pleasure it was to work with them. When a close friend, Mia Morris, mentioned the name Cy Grant in passing conversation, I had to stop her in her tracks and say "you mean THE Cy Grant?" You see, he was the first recollection I have of seeing a positive black person on TV – no backdrop to a Tarzan movie – no painted face black and white minstrel. If not for the likes of Cy Grant, there probably wouldn't be people like me who are now very much part of the fabric of British society, making huge economic and cultural contributions to make the United Kingdom a stronger and more vibrant place and proud of it.

Cy Grant is one of the people who has helped shape British and world history. The contribution of people like him from all parts of the Commonwealth to the peace and stability of the United Kingdom and our modern world is still yet to be fully acknowledged. Even after World War 2, he went on to shape the black presence in the UK through arts and entertainment. An inspiration for many young black Britons like myself.

Many want to forget that we had a colonial past. Most young people do not understand why we even have a commonwealth of countries, or indeed what the British Empire was? Many young white and black Britons still have no idea that black people have fought in every major colonial war since Empire began – in particular our contribution during and post World War 2. When celebrations and memorials take place how can many young black people feel British enough to take part in something when they see no reflection of themselves or their forefathers' and mothers' contribution to protecting the nation. As one of the greatest and most expansive empires in world history, it's not cool (as I hate to use the dreaded PC words) anymore to even talk of the British Empire. We are confusing our children and distorting our history. Well, I am a child of empire. There were still a lot of territories under the British flag when I was young and my parents (being from two of them) still spoke of helping the 'mother country' in her time of great need on the subject of World War 2. My mother more than anyone I know reinforced to me what being British is. And believe or not, she would have me up watching Cy Grant on TV and listening to his songs as part of my Caribbean / West Indian heritage also.

I was told by my uncle, who was in the RAF, that many black people fought in the war and that Cy and others fought for the right to be here. Racism on their return to the UK was rife! I was born in the east end of London and finding bombs on marsh ground whilst playing football or cricket was not uncommon. When I was at school I felt proud to join in the play ground war games and swap adventure war comics with friends (it didn't matter to me what colour my heroes were), but in history lessons my teachers used to say that it was OK to play games but in reality 'coloured people' (as we were called then) never took part in the war. Why? They couldn't find one picture or reference in their history books to substantiate a 9-year-old's claims. But then when Captain Scarlet came on TV in the late sixties, with the black Lieutenant Green, it was the first time I had seen a children's animated character that reflected our presence in this world positively. Again, it was Cy Grant. His voice relayed the commands to the members of Spectrum protecting Earth from the Mysterons. On many counts Cy Grant can be humbly called a 'hero'.

Britain's survival and growth heavily relied on men and women like Cy Grant; its colonies, people and resources. The Ministry of Defence has invested in an exhibition reflecting the contribution of these unsung heroes. Along with Cy you will see many of the other faces and stories as the exhibition begins to travel the country. A permanent exhibition in on show at the Royal Air Force museum in London.

History is important to us as a nation. It is at this point, as we lose more of the wartime generation, that we must protect their image and memories for the benefit of all in the United Kingdom and Commonwealth for years to come. We must re-define ourselves for the time we are in. A modern reflection. A wiser, more enlightened and richer Britain. None of our people should be forgotten or erased from history. When we stood together we defeated tyranny. We should now be proud to stand together and celebrate those who helped shape our history and the complexion of our society.

Terry Jervis
Jervis Entertainment Media Ltd
Merchandising Agent for the Secretary of State for Defence

1. Growing Up in a British Colony[4]

"I have been studying how I may compare
This prison where I live unto the world."
Richard II V.v.

I was born in the little village of Beterverwagting in Demerara in British Guiana (now Guyana), an independent and impoverished republic on the northeast coast of South America and part of the British Commonwealth. Its history is inextricably bound up with that of the West Indies and with the European expansion and domination, which started when Christopher Columbus thought he had 'discovered' the Indies. Even as a boy I was aware of the class structures and white privileges, but I too had been privileged in a country divided by race, class and the colonial system.

I grew up in the sleepy village for the first eleven years of my life and then in New Amsterdam, the capital of Berbice. Dutch place names are everywhere and the flat coastal strip with its canals looks much like a tropical version of Holland, without the windmills.

Yet it was the middle class values of British society that I was to inherit. My father was a Moravian minister and we lived in a huge manse with servants, next to an impressive wooden edifice of a church with an imposing steeple. The

---

[4] Chapters 1 & 2 are extracts from *Blackness and the Dreaming Soul.*

sound of church bells, choir practice and sermons blend in my memory with the song of kiskidees (*qu'est ce qu'il dit?*) and the tapping of woodpeckers on the tall coconut palm that swayed between the church and the manse, distant drumming (African and Indian) and the screams of my brothers and sisters, these suddenly ceasing at the approach of my father, a kindly but austere man.

We were brought up in a strictly Victorian manner – respect for our elders, correct behaviour, homework, piano lessons, Sunday School, morning service and outings to Georgetown to the Bourda cricket ground to watch West Indies play against Wally Hammond's England eleven. We were clean, respectful and proud. Like most of our 'class' we had household servants, but my mother always insisted that we kept our own rooms tidy and generally helped with the housework. My sisters sewed their own clothes, baked cakes and studied the piano. The household ran smoothly and life was very ordered indeed. Twice a week the house was filled with the delicious smell of baking bread and a healthy atmosphere prevailed. These are among my earliest memories.

Beterverwagting's two main roads ran north/south, parallel to each other. A canal ran alongside the road on the west, separating it from the land on which the church and manse lay and it was crossed by about six or seven bridges. You could walk, drive or cycle along the road or row along the canal northward towards the railway, which connected all the coastal villages between Georgetown, the capital and Mahaica, where you could take a ferry across the mile-wide mouth of the Berbice River to New Amsterdam.

~ A Member of the RAF of Indeterminate Race ~

As a small boy, together with other boys and girls, I would go swimming in a nearby creek, or visit a sugar plantation nearby called La Bonne Intention, from the days Guyana had been French. We would set out on day excursions in small boats along the canal system that led to the sugar refinery, negotiating the big iron punts laden with sugar cane which lined the final approaches to the factory, the heat, noise and smell of molasses pervading our senses. We were allowed to sample the molasses and chew the sugar cane by the black foremen in charge, returning home when it was beginning to get dark with tales of the dangers that lurked in the interior – the small bands of escaped slaves, who so many years after emancipation chose to live apart from the village as the Amerindians did. Whether there were still small bands of 'wild men' we were not to know, as I never saw any, but such bands of escaped slaves, men and women and their children, certainly did exist during the days of slavery and afterwards, and their memory still lived on in the minds of people when I was a boy.

Occasionally we would catch sight of an Amerindian or "Buck Indian", as they were derisively called. These were the true owners of the country who had been decimated by contact with the civilization of the white man; their 'simple' lifestyles scorned, their beliefs disregarded as no more than superstitions. Yet, like all the many and varied native people of the South American continent, they knew how to live in harmony with their environment, having a vast knowledge of plant and animal life, a knowledge the West is only now beginning to recognise and to respect.

But then we did not know a great deal about the indigenous peoples, nor for that matter did we know a great deal about ourselves, our origins, or who we were. My childhood had been sheltered; we assimilated the education we were provided and our morals and values were shaped by our upbringing. We knew little about our own parents' histories.

Fifty years after his death, my memories of my father are still strong and the quality of his life has challenged my own outlook and indeed my life experience. His strong character certainly influenced my character. I may not have realised just how much until recently, visiting my sister Valerie, I started asking questions about him and my mother. It seemed I knew little about their lives before their marriage. I had, of course, been aware that my father's father had come to the country from the island of Barbados and that my father had been a teacher before deciding to go into the ministry. He had met my mother whilst at the Moravian Theological Seminary at Buxton Grove on the island of Antigua.

As if to remind me that the only significant truth about my father was not to be found in his antecedents but rather in his life, my sister produced his bible, which she had somehow inherited. It had been my father's for most of his life, from the time he began his studies for the ministry until his death some forty years later; on the flyleaf was his signature, which had remained exactly the same throughout his life. The date: 1901.

To hold this book was like holding a sacred icon. It had been his daily companion, the pages discoloured and the edges frayed. It bulged slightly and the covers were in danger of coming apart. It had obviously been rebound to accommodate the vast number of additional pages that swelled its size by at least a fifth of what it had been, on which my father has made annotations, reflections and cross-references. My sister explained that my father had studied bookbinding at some point, hence the neatness and care commensurate with the reverence he had for it.

I had always held my father in some sort of awe, but holding this book so many years after his death, forcibly brought home to me just what an extraordinary person he had been. Now so many years on, I believe that this book deserves to be preserved and revered. It would provide valuable evidence for a thesis on Religion and Colonialism. It had been the cornerstone of his faith and of his ministry, a testament to a life of dedication and integrity.

With colonialism had come Christianity. It is ironic that those who brought it to the colonies no longer attend Church, whilst forms of Christianity flourish among the black community in England and also in 'darkest' Africa. For my father, Christian principles were the basis for all morality, service to the community and value within society, the very principles that formed the core of Moravian belief. The Moravians had been ruthlessly persecuted by the Church of Rome, and the leader of the movement for reform of the Roman Church, John Huss, had himself been burned at the stake.

My father's study had been crammed with books on every subject and on every wall from ceiling to floor; he hardly ever left it except to visit his parishioners or to take a service. I believe my love of books comes from the hours I spent as a boy browsing in this library whenever he was out. As well as the classics of English Literature and scholarship, it contained many books about black heroes and black achievement, material which had not been easy to come by in his lifetime. There was the poetry of Langston Hughes, whom I was to meet later in life in London, and of James Weldon Johnson and the writings of W.E. Du Bois. I also learned that the great Russian writer Alexander Pushkin and the French author Alexander Dumas were black, facts which are still not generally known today.

It was my father who introduced me to the exploits of the legendary Toussaint L'Ouverture, the great Haitian leader. One day he called me into his study, showed me a print of Toussaint and asked me to enlarge it. I fancied myself as an artist in those days and it was an honour to be asked by my father to do something for him.

Not only did his scholarship, his imposing presence for a shortish man, and his immaculate dress, hold me in awe, but it had been whispered that he had been born with a strange light birth mark in the shape of a cross on the dark skin in the centre of his chest and which faded as he grew older. I had never been able to verify this. In fact we never did ask enough questions of our parents, about his father and grandfather – what memories they may still have dating back to the days of slavery! Perhaps we did not want to know about slavery as if shame attached to the slaves for having been made slaves.

~ A Member of the RAF of Indeterminate Race ~

My mother was a great beauty and obviously well brought up as befits the daughter of someone of the privileged upper-middle class in a small West Indian island. Her father had been a Scotsman, a sergeant in charge of Prisons near English Harbour where, a century before, Nelson's Fleet had been fitted out on the island. She played the piano and indeed taught it to about grade 4 of the British School of Music. Most of us children were made to study the piano, but only the eldest, Ruby, attained any great proficiency, up to grade 8 I believe. My mother was also a competent painter in oils and water colour and did exquisite embroidery and crochet-work.

Despite the closeness of our family we somehow never got around to ask our mother about her childhood, or about her parents or how it came to be that she had Indian (from India) blood. We also never asked about our ancestry on the European side. We identified so much with the 'coloured' middle class that we had little curiosity about our ancestry on either side of our family tree.

My father was revered by all. A powerful orator, his sermons were masterpieces. He was also deeply concerned for the welfare of his local community, in particular the drainage and irrigation problems of our village, Beterverwagting, which was subject to frequent flooding,. He helped run a Farmers' Co-operative from an office under the Manse, and supported the political campaigns of local men, against the stranglehold of the plantocracy, to gain seats in the Legislative Council of the Colony.

He was fanatical about cricket. He had a stack of ball-by-ball score-books from all the major matches he had attended. He formed a cricket club in Beterverwagting, with a good pitch and pavilion and many inter-village matches were played. One of the rules of the club was that cricket must not be played on Sunday. One of my most vivid memories of him was when some people tried to break that rule. A very prestigious match was arranged between members of a visiting West Indian cricket team and a team from Guiana. When word got to him that this was taking place, he set off, after his sermon, for the ground armed only with his umbrella. He placed himself between the wickets and stood there all day in the boiling sun. There was no cricket on that Lord's day, that Sunday in Guiana. It was headline news in the papers the following day.

When I was about eleven years old the family moved to New Amsterdam, in Berbice, where my father was sent as minister for four Churches, two on either side of the Berbice River. This move entailed considerable changes in our lives. Before it, my elder brother and sisters had travelled to Georgetown from B.V (as Beterverwagting was known) for their secondary education. New Amsterdam was over sixty miles away and travel by the local railway, always a great adventure, was out of the question. Other arrangements had had to be made. Also my father's work load increased dramatically, and I was later made to accompany him on his frequent visits to his congregations in those remote outposts.

But New Amsterdam, although a small town, was very beautiful. Our new home was another huge wooden two-storied house in Coburg Street. The street was red-brick and shady, and the colour of the flowering trees, bougainvillea, and hibiscus and the wide range of fruit trees imbued a picturesque elegance to our new surroundings despite the fact that our house was opposite the Police Station and the Fire Brigade. I remember making friends with the Sergeant in charge of the Fire Brigade. He was quite a musician, playing the guitar in the typical Guyanese fashion with strong African influences. He also played the saxophone.

I had become increasingly bored with my piano lessons, the sounds of the guitar and saxophone seducing me away from the instrument. But my father would not hear of me taking lessons on either. I could learn the flute if I wanted, and the Sergeant was quite qualified to teach me. This seemed a good idea, as I was a bit young to start on the saxophone. It would also be a good introduction to playing a wind-instrument. But I found playing the flute extremely difficult, and when I realised that my father was expecting me to play in Church as soon as I was able to squeak out the simplest tune, I decided to call it a day. I did manage, however, to learn a few Chords and some bass rifts on the guitar from the Sergeant in between my futile attempts to 'lip' the flute.

One weekend, my younger brother and I and a few friends went swimming in the estuary of the Berbice River. Now this river is at least one mile across, and the currents around the Stelling quite strong at times. The end of the Stelling, where the twice-daily river-boat docked, protruded about a hundred yards from the bank. We rowed out from the side in a small boat towards the mouth of the river and dived off. Soon I found my-self on my own and caught up in a strong current. I made for the supporting posts of the Stelling. To my horror they were covered with barnacles, gleaming like broken glass, dark and green, and I knew I would cut myself to bits just trying to hold on against the whirlpool swirling round each post. There was nothing else to do but try to find a way out of the current and head for the boat a hundred yards away. I managed to pull away from the current, but found my strength failing; and panic was making it difficult to breathe. My brother and the others were some way off and I shouted for help. They seemed to think I was clowning!

I was unexpectedly and dramatically fighting for my life. Engulfed in the surge of my effort and my flailing arms, I felt it slipping from me, murky water everywhere, in my mouth, stifling my grunts, in my eyes and nose. The river was claiming me fast, my short life a blur before my eyes, as in a dream. Then, the merciful relief one feels on waking from a bad dream, a firm hand was under my chin supporting me as I was about to go down for the third and final time. I knew instinctively that it was my brother's. He had heard my shouts and had kept an eye on me just in case. Were it not for him I would not be telling this story. Unfortunately, over all the long years, I have seen very little of my brother. Our ways were to part shortly after our schooldays. We both were to become self-imposed exiles living away from the country of our birth, he in Scandinavia and me in England.

We attended Berbice High School in New Amsterdam, passing the Junior Cambridge and Senior Cambridge examinations, the same ones that were set for Secondary School pupils in England. Despite the fact that sitting next to me were boys of African, Chinese, Indian or Portuguese descent, the education we received implied that everything black was inferior. The only language we spoke confirmed this. History lessons told us nothing about ourselves or tried to explain the great diversity of our population. Slavery, the slave trade and the true nature of conquest and colonialism were never significantly dealt with. We learned about English Kings and Queens, the Wars of the Roses and the Napoleonic War. We learnt about English conquests, Nelson, the Armada, Magna Carta and Queen Victoria. We sang *Rule Britannia* every year on 24th May (Queen Victoria's birthday) and England was our Mother Country. We were never told about the civilizations in the New World that were destroyed by the Europeans. Columbus and Raleigh were heroes but we were made to think of some of our forebears as savages.

In geography we learned about London, Newcastle (that one does not take coal there), of the Pennines (the English ones, not the mountain peaks of Guyana and its magnificent Kaiateur Falls) and of Liverpool and Bristol (though not of the roles they played in the days of the slave trade).

In English we covered Shakespeare and Stratford on Avon, *The Merchant of Venice* (the disgusting Jew) and *The Tempest* of Prospero and Caliban. It was Oxford and Cambridge to which we all aspired; literacy in Guyana was once (but alas, not so today) among the highest in the world!

In Biology there was nothing of our own flora and fauna; we learnt the parts of a daffodil instead of the hibiscus.

Guyana was idealised by Sir Walter Raleigh, the English adventurer who had dreamed of discovering the City of Gold,

El Dorado. It was not until many years later that I began to reappraise our history and my relationship to it.

Raleigh had been released in 1505 from the Tower of London, where he was being held for treason, to go on an expedition to find the mythical city. In his book *The Discovery of the Empire of Guyana* (1596) he described this expedition claiming that the mythical city, supposed to be Manoa in the Guyanas, had "more abundance of gold than any part of Peru and as many or even more great cities". He was to lead two other unsuccessful expeditions between 1595 and 1616 but his dream was not fulfilled and in 1618 he was beheaded.

European expansion had started, in 1492, when Christopher Columbus set sail in search of gold and glory in the name of God and country. He was embarking on an outward journey into darkness that was to set in motion the destruction of cultures, civilizations, and of races and peoples on an unprecedented scale, setting the pattern for the eventual domination of the entire world by the European powers.

Over the ensuing years the conquest of the Aztecs and Incas took place and the greed and brutality of the Spanish conquistadores has been well documented. Many other civilizations perished and what the Spanish had started was soon eagerly taken up by the Portuguese, the British, French and Dutch. The scramble for new territories to conquer was to last for centuries.

Guyana was not as immediately attractive to the Spanish as their earlier conquests. Columbus had sailed along the low unattractive coastline on his third journey to the 'new' World in 1499, but did not make a landing. And although the Spanish landed a year later and occupied the region now known as Venezuela, it was the Dutch who first settled and colonized the eastern region.

Their first settlement, in 1616, was on an island some forty miles up the Essequibo River which they called Kykoveral (Look over all) near the Cuyuni and Mazaruni Rivers. Later the settlement spread North towards the flat coastal strip. In 1780 the Dutch colony was captured by the British who were in turn expelled by the French in 1783. A year later it was back in the hands of the Dutch. In 1795 a Republic was declared but this did not last long as the territory was again captured by the British in 1796. In 1802 it was returned to the Dutch by the Treaty of Amiens. A year later the British were back in power and in 1814 it was officially ceded to Britain. In 1831, the three colonies of Essequibo, Demerara and Berbice were united to form British Guiana. Immediately to the East lay Dutch Guiana(Surinam) and beyond that French Guiana(Cayenne). Venezuela to the West (originally Spanish Guiana), is still claiming about two thirds of the Country. Thus it is that even though the country is situated on the South American mainland, Guyana is considered part of the West Indies and shares with these islands a history of post-Columbian scramble for possessions which rapidly changed hands. Politically, culturally and economically their destinies are irrevocably intertwined. Their histories are chequered by conquests.

Guyana has many river systems and it derives its name from this fact (Land of many waters). With their intimate knowledge of low-lying lands, the Dutch were responsible for its irrigation and protection from an encroaching sea. The clearing of, and protection of agricultural lands was hard work and the introduction of slaves from Africa began with a Charter to the Dutch West India Company in 1621. The indigenous inhabitants, the Carib, Arawak and Warrau, usually referred to as Amerindians, were not considered suitable as they died like flies on contact with the settlers. It is no wonder that they were inclined to disappear into the forested interior.

All the European powers indulged in the despicable slave trade. The most barbaric atrocities were perpetrated and not surprisingly the slaves constantly revolted. The most famous slave rebellion in history, took place in Haiti, then St. Domingue, in the late 18th. Century. It led to the establishment of the first black Republic in the New World. My father had introduced me to the leader of that rebellion, Toussaint L'Ouverture, when he had asked me to enlarge his portrait.

My father's interest in black history and culture was to influence me greatly. In a period rich in remarkable men, Toussaint was one of the most remarkable. C.L.R. James, the great West Indian historian and man of letters, had this to say about him: "With the single exception of Bonaparte himself no single figure appeared on the historical stage more greatly gifted than this black man, a slave till he was forty-five."

But what is perhaps more significant is that there had been a slave rebellion in our own colony, Guyana, in Berbice, which preceded the famous one in Haiti by nearly 30 years, in 1763. It was led by Cuffy and the slaves were in complete control of the Colony for nearly a year before it was finally suppressed.

Slavery was to continue for almost two centuries. The trade itself was abolished in 1807 and the institution of slavery in 1833, not as is often suggested, for humanitarian reasons. Economic considerations were manifesting themselves more and more. But in order to fill the gap in labour which resulted after emancipation, a system of indentured labour was introduced initially from China, and from the Portuguese island of Madeira and later from India. So the population of Guyana comprises peoples from England, Holland, Portugal, Africa, India, China, a strange and exotic admixture of all these peoples and the indigenous Amerindian. It calls itself the Land of Six Peoples, which is not quite accurate. It is a land of great racial and cultural diversity.

Slavery had shaped every aspect of life, the social structure and the very psyche of West Indians. The mixing of tribes during slavery had disrupted families, social values and the communalism of the traditional African cultures. The slaves were mere chattels, brutalised and forced to work in the most appalling conditions, punished with the greatest bestiality, the women raped, the men disempowered. The effects of slavery on the West Indian black population was quite simply traumatic – the men folk betraying an ambivalence amongst themselves and towards white people who had suppressed and mentally castrated them – distrust of the white man and yet not showing it, and of those they do not know including other West Indians.

They were defined by patterns that were alien to their very being making them more divided, contemptuous of others and of themselves, jealous of those who oppressed them. As Frantz Fanon put it:

"Every colonized people – in other words, every people in whose soul an inferiority complex has been created by the death and burial of its local cultural originality – finds itself face to face with the language of the civilizing nation; that is, with the culture of the mother culture. The colonized is elevated above his jungle status in proportion to his adoption of the mother country's cultural standards. He becomes whiter as he renounces his blackness, his jungle".

I myself am only about four generations removed from slavery and a mixture of three racial groups, African, Asian and English. We were colonized in body as well as in mind and a strange darkness pervaded our souls. We divided ourselves into classes, as the English did, but based on shades of colour – the mixed races, the coloured, below the white English and Portuguese, but above the blacks and the Indians who were 'coolies' (we actually used the terms our masters used!). The policy of divide and rule was one of the most effective ploys developed by Colonial powers.

Attempts had been made to stamp out the African heritage. Africa was the continent of darkness and of 'brute beasts'. A country without a history of its own. Africa had contributed nothing to human knowledge, there were no civilizations there – Egypt, like Greece, was part of Europe! The

African gods worshipped, only in secret and in 'primitive' incomprehension. Slavery had obliterated the past. The early slaves had been split up into different language groups so they could not communicate. They eventually lost their language and their religious rituals were prohibited; and the drum, central in so many of the world's cultures, only permitted to be played on certain days. Boxing Day, with its masquerades, drumming and feasting had more significance to the African slaves than Christmas Day.

But Africa was not suppressed; it went underground and lived in the heartbeat of the black population. To their credit, black West Indians, like their African forebears, have retained a vestige of their lost values. But the loss of communality has resulted in an inability to organise effectively as a community. Individualism and going it alone became a trait of the West Indian personality. Only in moments of extreme crisis was there the need of coming together for the common good. But even here, individual ambitions frustrated the attainment of the desired goals. Economically disenfranchised, the black population was much later to gain political power, creating even more racial tension.

The Indians had come as indentured labourers. They too had their festivals, pujahs or tajahs, as we called them, with their elaborate, glittering towers that were carried through the streets to the sound of drumming, only to be thrown into the river at the end of the festivities. The Indians were industrious, working in the cane fields as the blacks before them, but then setting up shops and other enterprises. They still had their languages and their religious beliefs. Mosques mushroomed on the horizon, alongside Hindu temples and Christian Churches where the worshippers were mostly black.

Black and Asian people were not homogeneous and so inadvertently served the interests of the white ruling class. The colonial legacy had encouraged division, and has created confusion politically as well as in the economy. The hierarchical structure, which even after the Europeans had finally been ousted, had left its own value system as the cultural norm. Despite its many cultures, Guyanese had been educated to value only the culture of England, and so have lost their true identity as Sir Walter Raleigh, the would be discoverer of Guyana, lost his head.

In such a climate I grew up. Able to appreciate Bach and Beethoven and to recite Keats and Shelley. At the young age of ten or eleven I was made to recite *Ode to A Grecian Urn* by Keats at Speech Day at primary school in front of the whole school – children, parents and teachers. I remember how apprehensive I'd been. I hardly understood the words:

> *Thou still unravished bride of quietness*
> *Thou foster-child of silence and slow time,*
> *Sylvan historian, who can't thus express*
> *A flowery tale more sweetly than our rhyme...*
> *What leaf-fringed legend haunts about they shape*
> *Of deities or mortals, or of both,*
> *In Tempe or the dales of Arcady?*
> *What men or gods are these?*

I hardly understood the words: *Sylvan historian, Tempe, Arcady...* Obviously referring to an urn made in Greece. Little did I know at that tender age that the Greece Keats celebrated was linked in so many ways to ancient Egypt. That the Greeks, Diadoros, Danaos and Herodotus, the father of history himself, had recorded these links. But it is the last two lines of the final stanza that have stayed with me:

> *"Beauty is truth, truth beauty, that is all –*
> *Ye know on earth and all you need to know."*

Little did I then realize how those words would form the very basis for my search for meaning and become the root spur to me writing my book, *Blackness and the Dreaming Soul.*

Who accurately records our histories? For there are obviously many histories. What is truth and how do we perceive it? What is termed the truth may be shaped by language, culture and national bias.

I was to discover that perception is not only a faculty of the objective mind, but of a deeper participatory involvement in everything that exists.

I went for long walks in the Botanical Gardens and mused. Beauty and truth. I even had a poem, dedicated to "Poesy" published in the *Sunday Chronicle*. My father read it aloud to the entire family, my mother, my two brothers and four sisters, before Sunday lunch, after he had said grace.

My embarrassment was palpable.

I was to discover Aime Cesaire and blackness much later. My true education only began when I came to England and discovered that I was black and that England was not my mother country. After the initial shock came later the deep revelatory and healing potential of that discovery.

Today Guyana is still bedevilled by its past. Privilege and racial conflict have festered beneath the surface of political life. It is little wonder that as a young man I dreamed of going overseas to widen my horizons. I did not have any strong feeling of *querencia*, of belonging.

The coastal strip is flat and uninspiring and I never experienced the numinous quality of the interior, the untouched and primeval rainforests. My only visit into the heart of the country of my birth was a day trip to the Kaiateur falls, years after I had finally left it.

I have always envied Wilson Harris and his ability to create a meaningful mythology with his evocation of Colombian myths and of redemption in the collision of cultures; the brilliant tortured landscapes in the novels of Edgar Mittelholzer, my next door neighbour, who had been barred from visiting our home by my father for his frank anti-puritanical views; and A.J. Seymour's long poem *The Legend of Kaieteur* glorifying a dubious history; and all those who strove so hard to blend a distinct and unique Guyanese consciousness.

I could not turn my back on the classical music that had filtered through the house as a child nor the distant drumming, African and Indian, the banned Cumfa dances and the Indian tajah, and the Spanish music over the airwaves, all of which resonated in my soul; as did the sound at night of a lone guitarist accompanying a doleful African melody:

~ A Member of the RAF of Indeterminate Race ~

"Martha, sweet Martha, Martha, sweet Martha,
Tell me where you get that money from."

What was distinct about our culture was its diversity, but at that period of my life I did not appreciate the symbolic significance of this. The social, political and economic realities overshadowed any awareness of possible cultural synthesis or any real sense of belonging. To my young mind, the unbroken flatness of the physical landscape, along with a pervading sense of colonial stagnation, seemed to impose limits on my future innermost horizons. I had to escape.

Two years after the outbreak of war in Europe, the opportunity presented itself...

2. The Royal Air Force

By the outbreak of World War II in 1939, the Royal Air Force had changed its mind about the recruitment of 'men of colour' into its privileged ranks, and by 1941 it was even prepared to recruit them as aircrew!

[A year previously, a friend of mine, Sydney Kennard, son of an English doctor and his black wife, had applied to join the Royal Air Force but had been refused entry, even though he had a pilot's licence obtained in America and had paid his own fare to England for the purpose of joining up.]

The Air Force (Constitution) Act of 1917 restricted entry into the Royal Air Force to men of pure European descent. Although sections of the act permitted voluntary enlistment of *'any inhabitant of any British protectorate and any negro or person of colour'* in exceptional circumstances, no such 'aliens' were to be promoted above the rank of Non-Commissioned or Warrant Officer. This, despite the fact that during the First World War a Jamaican Sergeant Pilot Clarke and an Indian 2nd Lieutenant Indra Lal Roy had distinguished themselves in the Royal Flying Corps (see notes at the end of this chapter).

The RAF changed its policy regarding the admission of non-Europeans as a direct result of the loss of some 3,000 aircrew, sustained during the Battle of France and the Battle of Britain in 1940. Suddenly the doors were open for young men from the colonies, particularly from the West Indies, to enlist.

~ A Member of the RAF of Indeterminate Race ~

The glamour of flying with the Royal Air Force as a pilot was irresistible, never mind the supreme irony of the situation – the well documented[5] and historic racist recruitment policies of the British Armed Forces, even whilst waging a war against a racist Nazi regime.

Suddenly the cream of West Indian young men was being exhorted to apply to join the distinguished ranks of the Few. I was one of four of the first Guyanese to be selected to serve as aircrew, and how proud I was that I had passed A1.

My decision to join up had been prompted solely by a desire for adventure and to get away from what I foresaw would be a dull future in a British colony. I would not have been able to afford a University education even if that were possible during the war.

And so it was that I came to England in 1941 to join the Royal Air Force.

I was among the first batch of about 500 West Indians recruited as aircrew, as against about 6,000 as ground personnel. We sailed from Georgetown to Halifax, Nova Scotia, stopping off at various islands in the Caribbean along the way. We lay anchored in Halifax harbour for a few days as a convoy of ships gathered, before we set sail on the hazardous journey across the Atlantic. Whilst there, we witnessed a most spectacular display of the *Aurora Borealis* or 'Northern Lights', which occasionally occurs in the winter months at these latitudes; a constantly changing celestial display of

---

[5] Marika Sherwood, *The Colour Bar in the British Military Services 1939-45*, Many Struggles (London, Karia, 1985)

shimmering light – red, blue, green and violet – caused by the interaction between the solar winds and the earth's magnetic field. We stood there in the cold night air, transfixed by this extraordinary phenomenon of nature, a sight I was destined never to see again.

The passage lasted for many days in freezing weather, with a constant lookout for the U-boats that were causing so much havoc in the Atlantic. We were all pressed into service to stand watch, by day and by night. The night shift was the most arduous:– the dull, relentless throb of the engines as we tried to stay upright on the heaving deck, cold and damp from the freezing spray stinging our faces. How many ships were in the convoy? I had not the slightest idea. The ships kept a safe distance from each other in case of an attack. Fortunately, none occurred during the crossing and we arrived safely in England.

The first step in the recruitment process was being taken to the Receiving Centre for air crew at St John's Wood in London, a huge, towering building, reminiscent of some I'd seen in Halifax. We were soon kitted out. I was now an AC2, equivalent to a private in the Army. Soon I'd be an LAC or Leading Aircraftman, recommended to start training as a pilot. We wore a white flash in our caps, denoting that we were destined to be air crew, which gave us a great sense of pride.

I cannot recall exactly how long we stayed at St Johns Wood, but there was an incident which quite amused me. On one occasion whilst standing on guard duty outside the block, a middle-aged Englishman stopped to chat with me. He was polite and seemed surprised that I spoke English as well as he, albeit with my West Indian accent. Many were not aware that literacy in British Guiana then was much higher than in Britain. Also, the doctor who first examined me on arrival had expressed surprise at the toughness of my skin when administering the prescribed injection for servicemen from overseas.

The first Training Unit I was sent to was at Syerston, in Nottinghamshire, where we studied meteorology, navigation, the use of the navigational aid G, astronomy, Morse code, and learned to use simulators. All aircrew had to undergo this training. This was a good period. There was strict discipline but a relaxed and friendly atmosphere. There was no hint of colour prejudice. I met young men from all over England and there was a young Mauritian with whom I became very friendly. But we all went our separate ways after leaving and I never again saw any of that first batch of young LACs.

I had received exceptionally high marks in all subjects – in the high nineties for navigation.

Our next stop was Elementary Flying Training School (EFTS) at Ansty, near Coventry, learning to fly Tiger Moths. This was something special for a young lad fresh from the colonies. It was a heady experience but exhilarating – the rush of air in the open cockpit plus the noise of the Tiger Moth, which did not, however, dull one's senses to the wonderful scenery of the English countryside in good weather.

Learning to use the controls was really challenging, even though the instructor was extremely patient. We were supposed to be able to go solo after twelve hours flying time. I was beginning to feel that I could do with another couple of hours, but things were not to work out exactly as I had expected. About the time I was to do my first solo flight I was informed, that I had been selected to be a navigator. I would not be doing my solo flight, and so no Spitfire for me!

Despite my strong remonstrations, there was little I thought I could do without creating a great deal of unnecessary fuss. As the Commanding Officer said, "We're fighting a war, young man, and you volunteered."

I had excelled at navigation on my initial Aircrew training and because of this I was selected. This happened to many would-be pilots, but it was a bitter pill for those of us, like myself, who had volunteered from the colonies and who had been tempted by the sheer glamour of becoming pilots, even though it involved taking a calculated risk with our lives.

I would be trained as a navigator, most likely as a member of a bomber crew. The reason, not explained in any great detail, was that there was an urgent demand to adopt the new RAF policy to split the old 'Observer' trade into two specialized ones – navigators and bomb-aimers. Suddenly, for every bomber crew, another trade was required.

It was not until after the war that I was to l learn that the revision of air crew categories had been absolutely necessary for many reasons, the chief of which was the recognition that navigational standards had been unsatisfactory for precision bombing. Added to this, was the fact that Observers were under a great deal of stress, having the two-fold role of guiding the bomber to its target, as well as the dropping the bombs. By creating specialist trades, Navigators could concentrate on the job of reaching the target and returning to base, otherwise the whole mission would be jeopardised.

Navigational aids were improving all the time and navigation became a very specialised art. Having got to within sight of the target the bomb aimer would be free to concentrate solely on the task in hand. The safety of the crew was thus enhanced.

Every aircraft represented a huge investment; the lives of the crew and the many months expended on their training; the cost of production of the aircraft and the equipment on board (the bomb-load, guns, navigation and wireless aids, etc). A Lancaster consisted of 55,000 separate parts. It has been estimated that half a million different manufacturing operations were involved in producing just one Lancaster bomber!

Teamwork was seen as a key factor for the success of any operation and it soon became very clear that the navigator's role was as important as that of the pilot, even though this took some time to sink in. [In the Royal Air Force, pilots were the captains of the aircraft, the pin-up-boys. In the American Air Force the navigator was the captain.]

This raises another question. Why was it, that at this time, so few West Indians and West Africans volunteers were trained as pilots? [Ulric Cross, Johnny Smythe, Dudley Thompson, Ronald Hall were navigators, like myself] Some who made it as pilots, apparently experienced difficulties recruiting white crewmembers. When they did, as in the case of Warrant Officer Owen Sylvester, on being transferred to a new station the Commanding Officer had difficulty accept-

ing the situation, indicating that the reversal of RAF racial
policies in the recruitment of non-Europeans had obviously
owed more to expediency than to any genuine change in attitudes that had prevailed for centuries and are only now being
addressed.

I personally never experienced any racism in the RAF. I
had accepted the reason given for me to train as a navigator,
never suspecting that, in my case, it had been anything but
genuine. I still had not been subjected to any form of overt
prejudice. A war was on and I was wearing a uniform. People
were generally friendly. Outside in the streets I occasionally
heard a child say "Look, mummy, a black man!" That always
brought me up sharp. Before coming to England I didn't
think of myself as black – a quite salutary shock!

I was to realize that I was defined in a certain way 'at home'
and another in the 'mother country'. Coming to terms with
either label was to realize that I was an outsider – that white
people excluded people of any colour other than their own.
On walking into a saloon bar in the country, suddenly there
would be a deathly hush. It was as though I had suddenly
come from an alien planet.

Later, as an officer, there was a mild raising of eyebrows
when I first walked into the mess, but this soon turned to ac-
ceptance when I spoke the King's English, albeit with my
West Indian accent.

And so it was that I went on to train as a Navigator at No
2(O) A.F.U Millom in Cumberland in November 1942. This
also turned out to be quite challenging. We trained on An-
sons. One had to be quite meticulous in one's observations

with the navigation aids available and in plotting and evaluating changes in wind speed, which was always changing. There was never a let up at any time if you were to be successful. In night training flights I recall taking fixes from the stars to plot my position. I was never sure that my readings were absolutely up to scratch, but one did one's best and we always managed to complete the set itinerary and return to base. The astronomical and other training at Syerston had been worth its weight in gold.

One morning, at the height of winter, I awoke to find the landscape all covered in snow. It was dead still and the sunshine was crisp on the whiteness. It was a miracle, my first experience of snow and one I shall never forget. That same winter at another airfield, I spent a full day shovelling snow from the runways so that bombers could take off and land; backbreaking work, and just the opposite of that magical scene at Millom. Life is full of contrasts! I was beginning to understand the underlying duality of things within a non-dual reality.

I qualified as Navigator and Astronomical Navigator on 5 February 1943 and was told that I was being recommended for a commission. This news was extremely welcome and in some way compensated for my disappointment in not continuing my training to be a pilot. The Commanding Officer, no doubt aware of the RAF's previous policies about recruiting 'men of colour', said he was taking an unprecedented step in making the recommendation, but that it was fully deserved and that he would take full responsibility for the decision and that should I encounter any difficulties in future that I should not hesitate to get in touch with him.

In March I was posted to No 30 Operations Training Unit at Hixon, Staffordshire. Here I teamed up with my Captain, Flying Officer Alton Langille, a French Canadian who chose me to be his navigator as he was to choose all the other crew members – because we were the best at our respective trades among the new batch of air crew. They were three Englishmen, P/O Don Towers, radio-telegrapher, P/O Charles Reynolds, bomb aimer and Flight Sergeant Geoffrey Wallis, mid-upper gunner.

Our last flight at this unit, in which we trained on Wellingtons, ended in a crash landing on Greenham Common in the early hours of the morning of 5 May 1943 after a training flight across the English Channel to drop leaflets on Nantes. No one was hurt. We had an engine failure on the way back and we were warned by the Pilot that we would have to make a crash landing. I do not recall that there was any great panic. We all had great trust in Al. We landed with the nose of the Wellington up against the trunk of a very large tree and crawled out, completely unscathed, in the early morning of May 6th.

That same day we were picked up by another Wellington and flown to a Conversion Unit to train on the Lancaster Bomber. The Lancaster was to prove the most successful bomber during the ensuing months and indeed for the duration of the war. Pilots loved flying them and the navigator's station was well equipped with navigational aids. Here we acquired our last two crew members: P/O Joseph Addison, tail gunner, from Canada and Sgt Ronald Hollywood, Flight Engineer, from England. They were the only members of the crew who did not survive the war.

Less than two weeks later, on 19 June, we were ready for ops as members of 103 Squadron, stationed at Elsham Wolds in Lincolnshire, situated south of Hull, on the other side of the Humber. The aerodrome had been built on land that had once been a farm, after which it took its name.

This was the time of the massive bomber raids on Germany, known as 'the Battle of the Ruhr', which started in March 1943 and lasted until July. The objective was the 'progressive destruction and dislocation of the German military industrial and economic system' as well as the hoped-for demoralizing effect on the German people. After just one 6½-hour cross-country flight by night on 19 June, thus clocking up a total of one hundred and sixty three hours flying time, half of which were by night, we went on our first bombing raid to Mulheim on 22 June 1943.

As navigator one was kept continuously occupied. You did not see much of what was going on below. It may have been completely different for my pilot, having to fly the Lanc through all that flack, or for the gunners looking out for fighters, or indeed for all the other members of the crew. For myself, my sense of responsibility for getting us there and back was paramount, and that may be why the obvious dangers of the situation did not seem to get to me. In the Lancaster, the navigator's position, just behind the pilot, was screened off so that no light could escape to betray our aircraft's position to enemy night-fighters. In any event, whenever I had a peek, and that was only when we were over the target, I was only too happy to get back to my station to work out a course that would get us away from the scene; away from the noise of the battle, the flares, the searchlights, the inferno below, and the unnerving jolting of the aircraft whilst we were over the target.

Two nights later we took part in another raid, this time on Wuppertal. It was a surreal repeat of the first flight. I don't think aircrew were fully conscious of the havoc and destruction they were causing. All they were thinking was 'drop those bombs on the target and get out of there'. Warfare denudes you of your humanity. Yes, I had sought adventure, an escape from a dull future in a British colony, but reflecting on it afterwards, I feel no sense of pride.

In a sense I am grateful that we were destined to complete no further operations over enemy territory. Our next flight would be our last. The very next night, Friday, 25 June 1943, one of the shortest nights of the summer, 473 bombers from Bomber Command of the RAF (twin- and four-engine) attacked, among other places, Bochum and Gelsenkirchen in the Ruhr. A total of 24 Lancaster bombers from our Squadron were incorporated into the operations. Our Lancaster, W4827, was one of them.

At 22.42 hours the first of 24 planes of 103 Squadron took off for a rendezvous near Harwich on the East Coast of England. There we joined a large stream of bombers, which set out across the North Sea in the direction of the Ruhr. The excitement was intense.

~ A Member of the RAF of Indeterminate Race ~

I was to learn after the war that of the 24 planes from 103 Squadron, four had to return early to base. The remaining 20 proceeded towards the target. Our aircraft was trailing slightly behind the main force of bombers when we arrived over the already blazing target.

Even amidst the deafening drone of scores of other aircraft, the muffled explosions below, the glow of the target area, the flak, the sweeping searchlights and the sudden bumps as the aircraft rode the frenzied skies, I never questioned what I was doing there. I cannot remember feeling particularly frightened; the thought of imminent death did not cross my mind. It was as though we were in another state of consciousness, emotionally switched off yet our minds functioning clearly as we got on with the things we each had to do.

The navigator's station was immediately aft of the pilot's position, with a small table on the port side of the cabin on which sat the chief navigational aid – the Gee radio navigation system.[6]

---

[6] G short for "Grid" or AMES Type 7000 was a British radio navigation system used during World War II; the ideas in GEE were developed by the Americans into the LORAN system. LORAN was used by the US Navy and Royal Navy during World War II, and after the war came into common civilian use world-wide for coastal navigation, until GPS made it obsolete. GEE transmitters sent out precisely timed pulses. The aircraft using GEE, Bomber Command's heavy bombers, examined the time of arrival on an oscilloscope at the navigator's station. If the pulses from two stations arrived at the same time, the aircraft was an equal distance from both, allowing the navigator to draw a line on his map of all the positions at that distance from both stations. Similarly, a difference in the arrival times indicated that the aircraft was closer to one station than the other; the actual difference denoted a particular hyperbola along which the aircraft must lie.

On arriving over the target, we dropped our bombs from a height of between 19 and 20 thousand feet. Shortly after doing so we were hit by flack, which penetrated the bomb hold, leaving the fuselage on the other side, but without causing any further damage. A minute earlier and we would have had it!

We headed for home at an altitude of 21,000 feet, still trailing a bit behind the main stream of bombers.

Shortly afterwards, over Holland, the tail gunner, Pilot Officer Joe Addison, shouted over the intercom that a German fighter was closing in from underneath us. The German fired a long volley and a jet of tracer spat out towards us.

Addison, from his tail turret, returned fire immediately. During the exchange the fighter climbed a little and veered off to the right. This manoeuvre brought him into the field of fire of the mid-upper gunner, Sergeant Geoffrey Wallis, who immediately opened fire.

Everything was happening very fast. All hell had broken loose. Flying Officer Alton Langille, the pilot, pushed the nose of the heavy plane into a dive...

In a moment the world was turned upside down. With the sound of the vicious cannon-fire from our attacker and of our two gunners returning his fire, Al, took evasive action. Then, surprisingly, as suddenly as it all began, every thing was normal again. The German fighter was nowhere to be seen.

Our gunners must have shot it down!

By making similar measurements with a third station, an additional hyperbola could be produced, leading to a fix at the intersection of the two lines.

"Great work, guys!" the Canadian accent of the skipper betrayed both the strain we were all under and the relief.

He levelled out, the plane behaved normally and no serious damage had been observed. Wallis was missing one of the covers of his ammunition boxes next to him, shot away during the attack. But none of us had been hit. With our spirits high again, we were soon lulled into a false sense of security...

The pilot checked our position with me. Despite the evasive action I had a good idea of where we were. The attack had occurred shortly after we were over Holland on route to our base at Elsham Wolds. We should be somewhere south of Amsterdam, near the small town of Haarlem. In half an hour we would be back.

But once again our peace of mind was to be short-lived.

This time it was the mid-upper gunner's voice over the intercom that shattered our complacency.

"Starboard outer afire, Skipper!"

So we'd been hit after all! But the fire was only a small one and we never thought for a moment that we would not make it back to base. We dived steeply, in an effort to smother the flames, but when we levelled out they had spread to the dingy stored below the starboard wing. However, we dared not jettison it for fear that the slipstream would take it onto the tail-plane.

Then one of the wheels of the undercarriage fell away in a flaming circle...

Now, we *were* up against it! Without our dingy we could not ditch in the sea in the event of the plane breaking up before we could cross the channel; and even if she did last that long we'd have to face a crash landing in England, and who knew where we might be forced to set down!

The situation was tense and worsening as each moment went by. By the time we reached the coast, we were a flaming comet over the Dutch sky. Both wings were afire now and I gave the shortest course to the English coast.

Unfortunately, we were flying into a headwind of about 80 miles an hour at 20,000 feet.

Undaunted, we unanimously decided to risk getting across the Channel rather than turn back and bail out over enemy-occupied territory. But it was becoming extremely difficult for Al to control the aircraft and he sensed that we would not make it across the channel. He decided to turn back over land.

No sooner had he got her round than he was forced to make another decision.

"Well, guys, this is it. Bail out and good luck! Get to it!"

Our nose had gone down again and there was no other option. I moved forward towards the hatch in the bomb-aimer's compartment...

I had never contemplated being in this situation. We had been instructed in the use of parachutes but never had to practise leaving an aeroplane by one. When I went forward I found that the bomb aimer and engineer, who should have already left in that order, were still fighting to free the hatch-door, which was situated underneath the bomb-aimer's cushion in the nose of the plane.[7]

Al, my pilot, seeing me go forward, left his controls and came after me. The four of us were soon piled one on top the other, tossed from side to side in the cramped space of the nose of the plane. Though not comprehending why we were unable to escape the now fiercely burning plane, I do not recall any sense of fear or panic. We seemed locked in a timeless moment of inertia when suddenly, with a deafening blast which lit up everything, our craft blew up and disintegrated, freeing us from each other – a free-fall into Eternity.

---

[7] I was to learn later that the difficulties we experienced with the forward escape hatch were replicated that very night when the crew of my own 103 Squadron faced similar problems. Alan Egan's crew were hit by flak near the target with similar results. It is now a known fact that the survival rate of air crew on Lancasters, was around eleven percent as opposed to twenty-nine percent of Halifax crews in similar circumstances. On Wellingtons the survival rate was just over seventeen percent.

When I recently visited the RAF Museum in Hendon and stood beneath the mighty nose of a Lancaster, I was amazed to see the actual size of the forward escape hatch, approximately two feet by three feet! With our parachutes on our backs and the plane tilting at a steep angle, it would have been impossible, it seems, to have escaped through it. It would appear that the Air Ministry were made aware of the hazard and pressured to do something about it, but alas, nothing was done until it was too late – a few months after the end of the war Lancaster bombers were fitted with a new larger escape hatch The raison d'etre of Bomber Command was that air crew might have been tempted to abandon their craft prematurely, instead of striving to bring them home to base! But the case of the faulty front hatch was probably the only flaw in construction of the greatest bomber of World War 2.

On reflection I realise that the whole sequence lasted for less than 30 seconds.

I found myself swallowed up by the silent stretches of space... My chute opened readily and I felt a sudden jerk and the strain of the harness on my shoulders as the wind snatched at the canopy, buffeting and tugging at it so that I swayed violently from side to side.

Except for the rush of the wind I was now in an unreal world of mist and utter silence. It was quite light up there above the clouds, which stretched like a white ethereal sea below. To add to the unreality, it seemed as if I was suspended in the air, for at first I experienced no sensation of falling.

The canopy of my parachute spread above me like a sinister shadow and I felt as if I were being borne swiftly aloft in the claws of a gigantic eagle.

I became aware of distant searchlights and the glow of a fire far below me. Our aircraft?

It still seemed that I was drifting aimlessly, with only the sound of the wind swelling the silk of the chute above me. Then came the sudden rush of a shadow coming towards me at immense speed. It was the ground reaching up to gather me.

Instinctively, I grabbed for the release knob on my harness, turned it and slapped it hard. The next thing I knew I was running on firm ground with ghostly, billowing folds of silk collapsing all about me.

Amazingly, I had made a perfect landing.

I wriggled out of the harness, my heart throbbing loudly. A glance at my watch showed that it was 2.38am. This was

June 26, one of the shortest nights of the year. It was already quite light and I could see that I had landed in an open field. The countryside was flat, with canals everywhere, reminiscent of the country districts of Guyana. I recalled that Guyana had been a Dutch colony before the British acquired it.

It was deadly quiet except for the barking of dogs in the far distance. The Germans were obviously searching for us. I knew I had to get away... fast.

"Head South," that's what they had instructed us to do if ever we found ourselves in this predicament. "Travel by night."

We had been given maps of the continent printed on silk handkerchiefs and a few other aids in case we did have to bale out. We were to head south and contact the British Consul in Spain, who would make speedy arrangements to get us back to England and back onto operations.

How I looked forward to that!

Then I remembered that I had to hide my parachute. It must not fall into the hands of the Germans. I started folding it up as I retraced my steps.

To my horror, and then relief, I found that I had landed just a few feet from the side of a huge ditch, a dyke, I supposed. What a baptism I had missed! In my bewildered state it might have proved fatal.

The soil by the bank was soft, but I do not think I made too good a job of hiding my chute. I was in a hurry and it was bulky. I recalled seeing them being packed, neat and compact.

~ A Member of the RAF of Indeterminate Race ~

Was I imagining it, or was the sound of men and dogs getting closer? I decided that would have to do.

For a while longer I stopped to gather my thoughts. And so it was that I found myself standing like Ruth among the alien corn (or was it oats?). I estimated that that I should be somewhere in the region of the small town of Haarlem – I could not have missed that name on my navigator's map.[8]

Trust me to land near a place where the colour of my skin would not matter! Definitely a good omen. But I also knew that I would be well within the coastal defences, where the Germans would be highly concentrated.

Yes, I'd better get on with it, head southeast, away from the coast. The Germans would be picking up our trails by now...

I wondered what had happened to the other members of the crew; had they survived the blast? Would I link up with one or more of them?

I walked, ran and trotted, but my legs and lungs were giving out with the stress of the situation. I prayed that the plane had crashed north or west of where I had landed, for I presumed that the Germans would commence their search for us from that point outwards. It would have been ironic if in trying to evade them I was, in fact, running straight into their arms.

The sounds seemed to be getting dimmer. I came suddenly to the edge of a field I had entered. A road bordered the field. Could I risk crossing it? It was already getting light and I

---

[8] According to Joost Klootwyk's reconstruction of the events of that night I had landed a few metres east of the Kagertocht (Kager track) on land owned by a Mr Bulk in Sloterweg, now Rijnlanderweg [Rhineland Road].

knew that I could not move about during the daytime. Then I heard the sound of a motor approaching and a vehicle of some sort went by – Germans, I figured, hot on our trails!

That settled it. I was already very tired, even though I had not travelled very far. I would not be attempting to travel until I had got some rest and grub. For the time the fields of what I thought of as oats were high enough to provide good cover.

This part of the country was very open. There were only isolated farmhouses in small clusters with a main road separating them. I considered whether it was time to strip off my badges of rank and trade, but decided against this. After all, there was no way I could pass as a Dutchman in the event of being caught. I opened my survival kit and distributed its contents into the pockets of my uniform. My plan was to spy out the land from my hideout behind the tall oats, to rest during part of the day and, when an opportunity presented itself, to try to contact a friendly Dutchman.

I watched the sleepy Dutch village awaken. I wondered if they were aware of what had been taking place over their heads whilst they slept, if they were indeed able to sleep with all the activity above and below. I was to learn many years later that an engine from our Lancaster (No. W4827) had fallen through the roof of a nearby farmhouse, killing the wife of a farmer.

As it grew lighter, a sense of *déjà vu* suddenly overwhelmed me. Had I been here before? I was to get this feeling later on when I was in a prisoner-of-war camp. But now it could have been because of the familiarity of the Dutch countryside. It reminded me of the country districts of Guyana, low-lying and flat, with canals everywhere. The village in which I was born was probably laid out by Dutch colonists before the British acquired it – it even had a Dutch name, Beterverwagting. Later I grew up in a town called New Amsterdam, which I left in order to come to England to join the Royal Air Force.

Here there were the same early morning sounds – a cock crowing, in the distance a man shouting, the bark of a dog, the sound of a pail clattering to the ground – simple every day sounds that made it hard to believe that only a few hours ago an air-battle had taken place overhead or that a war was in progress.

Then I heard the sound of something moving along the main road. I peered from behind the shafts of oats. It was my first sight of the enemy; a German soldier, cycling along the road, whistling, blissfully unaware that I was lying only about 10 yards away.

It was a long and frustrating day. It started to rain mid-morning and I got soaked, thus making it impossible to grab some sleep. I was already cold and cramped, lying on the damp earth. Then, as suddenly as it had begun, it stopped raining, only to start again about an hour later.

I was wet, miserable and hungry, but I dared not come out into the open, there were too many people milling about. I thought I should first approach someone who was alone to ask for help. I needed some grub and to know my exact position and where the Germans were stationed; I also needed somewhere to stay overnight – a barn would be ideal – there were certainly many around.

By mid-afternoon my spirits were very low. The day seemed terribly long. It was, after all, the 26 June.

Still no sign of any members of my crew. Had they survived? The thought kept recurring. Would it be easy for me to pass as a field labourer? Definitely not. I realised that I would have to move by night unless befriended by a Dutchman.

Crawling on my hands and knees, I had explored the area on three sides of the field. I was leaving a long muddy trail behind me and I was covered in mud. The road adjoining the field ran north-east to south-west. I would have to cross it at some time. To the east were a few small houses and a large barn within fifty yards of the ditch adjacent to where I hid. To the southwest and about 500 yards away was a huge solitary building. It was from that direction that the soldier on the bicycle had come and I suspected this very big house might be full of Germans.

Early in the evening the workers were coming home and things were settling down at last, although it was still bright.

Looking about me, I was suddenly aware of the opportunity I had been waiting for. He was alone in a plot of land adjacent to mine and well away from the main road. I crawled on my stomach towards him. When I was near enough I made small pellets of mud and threw them at him. The expression on his face as these started to drop about him was a poem of bewilderment. He looked upwards, caught himself and then looked about him.

Then he saw me. He must have recognised me for an air-man immediately, for he beckoned to me to move further way from the road and proceeded to do likewise himself. In a minute or so, he signalled to me to jump the six-foot ditch that separated us.

I threw myself at the other bank and clambered up to the man. He thrust a shovel towards me and immediately I knew I was in safe hands. From the road we'd just be two workers. He spoke no English, but showed me where I was on the silk-en escape map I held out to him. I was not far from where I expected to be; south-east of Haarlem, in a place near Nieuw-Vennep.

I intimated that I was famished and he nodded and led me to the big barn behind the nearest farmhouse. Suddenly I was the centre of attraction for a group of farm people and their children. A shot-down airman would always arouse people's curiosity, but there was something else here. I had encountered a similar kind of curiosity in parts of England where the natives had never seen someone of my colour close-up.

It wasn't going to be easy for me to escape...

But these Dutch country folk were warm and helpful, par-ticularly the farmer's wife, who was young, about my own age and very pretty. She took me to the cottage and attended to the wound I had sustained to the side of my head. Then she made me a hot meal, so when the interpreter arrived my spir-its had risen considerably.

He was a small, nondescript man in an ill-fitting pinstripe suit. His English was fairly good and he was able to translate all the questions the villagers put to me. They were anxious to know when the invasion would begin. They seemed to think it was long overdue.

"How long before it will commence?" they asked of me, as if I was the War Office.

I thought I should give them some hope so I replied,

"Soon now... it will not be long before your country will be yours again."

That seemed to cheer them up; they turned excitedly to each other. My plight was forgotten by all except myself and probably the interpreter, for he soon broke the bad news.

I had asked him to find out from the farmer whether he would permit me to sleep in the loft of the barn that night and the following day, as I was too tired to attempt to move that night. It was only then I was told that if the Germans did not already know of my presence at the farm, the chances were that they were certain to find out. I had been seen by too many people, any of whom might be a quisling.

He told me that if they did not hand me over, the farmer and his wife would be shot. I caught the look in the eyes of my benefactors. They were obviously distressed by the grim choices that faced them.

This came as a great blow. I pleaded that I simply had to get away, that surely everyone there could be trusted. I looked about me, they all seemed so concerned for me, but I also detected concern for their own safety. The interpreter told me of cases where people had been shot in the past for helping Royal Air Force personnel.

Nevertheless, I found it very hard to resign myself to literally giving myself up and asked the interpreter to help me find another way out, but all he said was that it was "quite impossible under the circumstances".

My frustration was complete. I knew that he had no choice in the matter. The sudden arrival of a Dutch policeman settled it. I was not aware that he had been sent for, but suddenly he was there, a large, amiable man who beckoned me to follow him outside.

There was nothing else to do. Turning to thank the farmer and his wife for their kindness, I followed him out. He motioned to me to occupy the pillion seat of his motorcycle and soon we were speeding along a very lonely country road.

Sitting there behind this friendly policeman, I did not quite grasp the fact that he was about to hand me over to the Germans. His manner was so warm and comforting that I entertained the irrational hope that he was helping me to escape in some way. But at the same time I was feeling emotionally drained and apprehensive. I was still in a state of shock from the events of the past 20 hours and was becoming resigned to my fate.

Then I became aware of the huge revolver protruding from its holster by his side. It seemed to be inviting me to grab it. It would have been very easy. Perhaps my friendly policemen was inviting me to do just that? All sorts of thoughts were going through my mind then. Was I up to it? I was not a very tough individual and I did not know how to ride a motorcycle. Even if I could, would it not be too conspicuous a way of getting about?

My speculations were short-lived. At that moment, he turned his head towards me, smiling, and said something that I did not understand. It could have been, "I wouldn't try that if I were you..." His nonchalance was off-putting. He must have known it would have been easy to disarm him.

Soon we were passing houses and the road was no longer deserted. We were entering a beautiful and quaint little Dutch village. I would not have expected the policeman to take me to his home, but this is exactly what he did. His wife made tea, and a teacher who spoke English and lived nearby by was called over. The daughter of the house put on a pretty frock. They were the essence of hospitality.

I gathered that I was to be called for by the Germans. They were very sorry about that. Meanwhile they went out of their way to be pleasant and to ask again about the Invasion. They kept a short-wave radio upstairs and fetched it to show me. They listened to the BBC every night.

It was still light when the Germans arrived to fetch me. There was a screech of brakes, a big Ford V8 pulled up and two *gefreiters* entered the house. They were matter-of-fact and abrupt. They exchanged hardly a word with the policeman. I was frisked and led out to the car. Soon we were driving along the same country road I had come along behind the policeman, but this time in the opposite direction.

We arrived back at the farmhouse from where I had been fetched and one of the soldiers got out. The farmer and his wife came out, as if expecting this, and stood before their front door. The soldier unceremoniously pulled out his revolver and started shouting at the two people who had befriended me. I felt terrible. Was he going to shoot them then and there? The man and his wife started speaking together. They were violently denying something. I do not know the German word for parachute, but it suddenly occurred to me that perhaps that was what the soldier wanted. The parachute was made of silk and would be very valuable, I thought.

To my relief the soldier put away his gun and soon we were off again, but for a brief second my eyes had caught those of the young wife who had been so concerned for me, and I knew that she would have run the same risk all over again if need be.

And thus my captivity began...

Caterpillar Club[9]

descent
soundless through the night
seemingly floating nowhere
amid ethereal mists and cloud...
vaporous, vanishing...
silent as in a frog-absent, noiseless night.
But still the ear vibrates
re-echoing the noise of battle
the urgency, the shriek, the shout, the BLAST!
then the sudden plunge, noise-deafened
into space;
the pounding of the heart
the gasp for air
the sprawling somersault
abreast the soft expanse of space;
the sudden check
harness straining hard on crotch;
the lurching swing ...swing ... swing...

descent
soundless and unending
as an unchallenged dream
beneath are open floating chutes
and way beyond the Earth
ethereal in the night's poor light;

---

[9] Airmen who save their lives by parachute are entitled to become members of the Irvin & Co. Caterpillar Club.

~ A Member of the RAF of Indeterminate Race ~

our aircraft burning in a small red glow;
a searchlight languidly sweeping and retreating
in the stillness of the night.

descent
soundless through the night
seemingly floating nowhere...
shadow looming, looming, looming
sudden sprung from shadow light
speeding upward, reaching, growing:
release box! turn! slap!
The Earth'll receive you.

Curtains...
a field in Holland
graceful folds of swooning silk...

Epilogue

After the war, I received a letter from Joost Klootwyk, a Dutchman who was 14 years old on the night that we fell from the skies. He had set himself the formidable task of learning as much as possible about the air battle over Holland that night and the operation that resulted in the crash of a Lancaster from No.103 Squadron based at Elsham Wolds on the night of 25/26 June 1943 in a field not far from his village. He had consulted all the records in Holland and in the Air Ministry, he had written to all my crew members and managed to put together an extraordinary record of the events immediately before and after the crash. I acknowledge that I have drawn on this record for some of the details of the events I have recounted about that fateful night.

I was also to learn that the local people remembered me very well indeed and about their reaction to my sudden appearance amongst them.

The burning wreckage of our plane came down to earth at 03.08 hours on the morning of June 26 on farmland a few miles west of Nieuw-Vennep in the Haarlemmermmeer. One of the engines from our aircraft fell through the roof of a farmhouse, killing the wife of the farmer.

Klootwyk had spectacularly fulfilled his boyhood promise by successfully contacting the Squadron for details of the mission that had traumatized his village. He was able to trace the number of the bombers that joined in the massive onslaught on the Ruhr that night.

~ A Member of the RAF of Indeterminate Race ~

"On the night of Friday 25 June 1943 the RAF had again planned an attack on the Ruhr area. For that attack, 474 bombers had been detailed of which 214 were Lancasters, 134 Halifaxes, 73 Stirlings, 40 Wellingtons and 12 Mosquitoes. Bomber Command was going to suffer heavy losses during that night, which also became on of the darkest pages of the air war over the Netherlands.

"24 Lancasters from 103 Squadron were detailed for the attack on Gelsenkirchen. One of the Lancasters was W4827 piloted by the Canadian F.O Al Langille. The crew consisted, apart from Langille, of navigator P/O Cy Grant (British Guiana), radio-telegraphist P/O Don Towers (England), bombardier P/O Charles Reynolds (England), flight engineer Sgt Ronald Hollywood (England) and gunners Geoffrey Wallis (England) and P/O Joseph Addison (Canada).

NOTES:

Internal Air Ministry correspondence and memoranda dating from 1945, cited in Roger Lambo, *Achtung! The Black Prince: West Africans in the Royal Air Force, 1939-46*. See also David Killingray, ed, *Africans in Britain* (Frank Cass and Company Ltd., 1994).

Letter from Roger Lambo to the author:

"The published notes Nos. 44 and 45 include the most damning quotes – PRO AIR 2/13437, entitled "Enlistment in the Post-War Air Force: Nationality Rules, 1944-51". My comment here was that this evidence "serves as a disturbing testimony of bigotry and deceit. In this regard, the memorandum of 16 August 1945, written by Air Chief Marshal Sir John C. Slessor, then the Air Member for Personnel on the Air Council takes the prize. His comments on the unsuitability of the gentleman with a name like "U-ba or Ah Wong", or who "looks as though he had just dropped out of a tree" are shocking, coming as they did, from a man of such stature." In note No.45 I refer to a memo of 23 August 1945, held in PRO AIR 2/13437, in which the Air Ministry agrees to drop the colour bar but to allow a process of national selection to run its course. As such "on paper coloured troops (would) be eligible for entry to the service, but the process of selection (would) eliminate them".

The papers were a real eye-opener for me and clearly indicated the extent of racial bigotry amongst high ranking service chiefs. As reported in my article, these comments, which were made towards the end of the Second World War ran counter to evidence of the general harmony that existed between aircraft crew members, irrespective of their individual race and to the excellent contribution made by West Indians and West Africans in the RAF.

My RAF flying career

- 1941 – induction at St John's Wood Receiving Centre
- Syerston Notts – meteorology, navigation, G, astronomy, morse code, simulators
- EFTS Anstey, Tiger moths – pilot training
- No.2 AFU Millom, Cumberland: 72 hours flying time, navigational training
- Commissioned
- No.31 OTU, Hixon, Staffs. Wellingtons. Crewed up
- Flight to Nantes – leaflets / crash at Greenham Common
- Conversion Unit – Lancasters
- 103 Squadron, Elsham Wolds
- 3 operational sorties: [during the Battle of the Ruhr: March 1943 – July 1944]
  - June 22, 1943 – Mulheim
  - June 24, 1943 – Wuppertal
  - June 25, 1943 – Gelsenkirchen

Total: 163 flying hours.

Our Mess [where we cooked, ate, lived and slept] at Lukenwalde, 1945.

Our Bunk beds at Lukenwalde, 1945.

POW Soup Detail at Lukenwalde, 1945.

POW recreation ground at Lukenwalde, 1945.

Russians soldiers liberate Lukenwalde, 1945.

Captured German prisoners at Lukenwalde, 1945.

The arrival of American troops at Lukenwalde, 1945.

American tents in winter at Lukenwalde, 1945.

Chapel built by Russian prisoners at Lukenwalde.

Americans cook-up.

German grave of unknown British aircrew.

50 years later – author at Sagan POW Museum 1993.

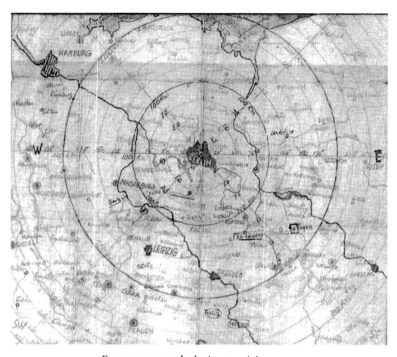

Escape map made during captivity, 1944.

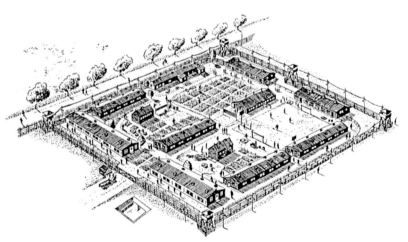

A GENERAL VIEW OF THE CAMP AT BELARIA.

Plan of Belaria – British Officers POW Camp.

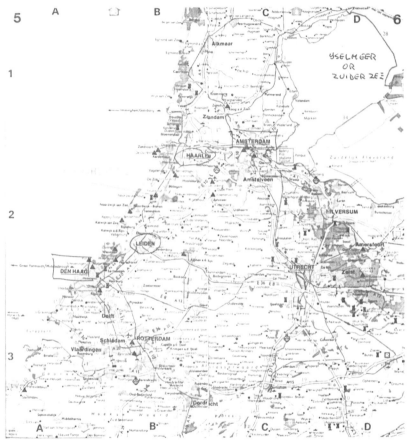

Map of Holland showing where our plane was shot down.

103 Squadron Lancaster about to take off on an op, Elsham Wolds 1943.

Navigator's station – interior Lancaster.

Crest of 103 Squadron.

Two stills from 'Sea Wife', 1956.

Cy on the front cover of Radio Times, 1957.
(photograph by Anthony Armstrong-Jones)

With Cliff Michelmore on BBCtv's 'Tonight', 1957.

Another photo by Anthony Armstrong-Jones, 1957.

'Calypso', 1958.

'At the Earth's Core' with Doug McClure, 1972.

'Shaft in Africa', 1973.

'Blake's Seven', 1979.

Cy in 2006.

Cy with Lance Corporal Johnson Beharry VC, 2009.

3. Prisoner of War

I was taken at first to a holding unit in Amsterdam for questioning. I was taken along a narrow corridor to a room where I presumed I was to be interrogated. On one side sat a line of prisoners. Suddenly, one jumped to his feet and rushed towards me. It was Geoff Wallis, our mid-upper gunner. He was looking tense and haggard, but very happy to see me. We grasped each other and I asked if he had any news about the other members of our crew. He was just able to blurt out that the engineer, Ron Hollywood, and the tail-gunner, Joe Addison were killed, but that he did not know about the others, when we were pushed roughly apart and I was led off.

But the Germans had found out something about the two of us – that we were members of the same crew.

They were to question me for a very long time. But I only gave my name, rank and number. I was led away and locked up in a cell with only one small window with iron bars.

There was a naked electric light bulb hanging from the centre of the ceiling, which was always on. The door was briefly opened to allow food to be passed to me. For breakfast I received an insipid beverage – I could not tell whether it was supposed to be coffee or tea – and a slice of very coarse brown bread; for the midday and early evening meals a bowl of soup, which also defied analysis. I wolfed it all down, as I was ravenously hungry.

The days dragged on and all I did was listen to the sounds coming from the courtyard outside the small window or doze off. I was to stay in solitary confinement for five whole days. Every other day I was taken out briefly to be interrogated but I found it easy to stick to my guns and say no more than I had said on the first occasion. I was never threatened with any form of torture, though I always imagined that that time would inevitably come.

Then one day I was dragged out into the bright sunshine and made to sit on a chair in order to be photographed. That was all. I was then led back to my cell to wonder what use would be made of that photograph. Perhaps it was just routine.

On the morning of the sixth day I was taken out of the cell and driven with scores of other prisoners to the main railway station. My mid-upper gunner was nowhere to be seen, perhaps because he was a sergeant.

We were put aboard a train and gathered that we were being sent to a prisoner of war camp. It was a big relief to be amongst other airmen and no longer in solitary confinement.

The trip by rail lasted the best part of two days. There were frequent stops.

Stalag Luft 3, near Sagan on the River Bober in Silesia was one of the largest German prisoner-of-war camps for aircrew personnel. It was famous for the largest mass escape ever to leave taken place, known as the 'Wooden Horse' escape, and later for the dastardly shooting of fifty Royal Air Force Officers after another massive breakout – the Great Escape – in March 1944.

My arrival at the camp created a bit of a stir amongst the Germans. A black officer! The Commanding Officer sent for me. I was ushered into the presence of a very handsome middle-aged man, not the type of man one would have expected to see in charge of a prisoner of war camp. He had an intelligent, dignified manner and was extremely polite to me. He asked me where I came from and thrust a page of a German newspaper in front of me. It featured the picture of me, taken after five days of solitary confinement.

Fame at last! There I was, staring scared and suspicious out of the page over the caption, *Ein Mitglied der Royal Air Force von unbestimmbarer Rasse* (A member of the Royal Air Force of indeterminate race). The name of the paper was the *Völkischer Beobachter*.[10]

I still have the cutting from the paper he gave me, which is reproduced on the following page.

---

[10] The *Völkischer Beobachter* (Völkisch Observer) was the newspaper of the National Socialist German Workers' Party (NSDAP) from 1920. It first appeared weekly, then daily from February 8, 1923.

The "fighting paper of the National Socialist movement of Greater Germany" (*Kampfblatt der nationalsozialistischen Bewegung Großdeutschlands*) had its origin in the *Münchner Beobachter* (Munich Observer), which in 1918 was acquired by the Thule Society and in August 1919 was renamed Völkischer Beobachter. The NSDAP purchased it in December 1920 on the initiative of Dietrich Eckart, who became the first editor.

The circulation of the paper was initially about 8,000 but increased to 25,000 in autumn 1923 due to strong demand during the Occupation of the Ruhr. In that year Alfred Rosenberg became editor. With the prohibition of the NSDAP after the Beer Hall Putsch of November 9, 1923, the paper also had to cease publication, which resumed however on the party's refoundation on February 26, 1925. The circulation rose with the success of the Nazi movement, reaching more than 120,000 in 1931 and 1.7 million by 1944.

At the end of April 1945, a few days before the German surrender in World War II, the *Völkischer Beobachter* ceased publication.

Ein Mitglied der Royal Air Force von unbestimmbarer Rasse

Author's photograph as it appeared in the
German propaganda newspaper Völkischer Beobachter.

On winds of war I've soared
and spread my wings;
alas,
the prison pebble in my craw
has grown too big.
earthbound,
I crawl and flap around
horizons narrowed
a snared stag
heart arrowed
or violin with broken strings;
and I recall
circling crows
gracefully and slowly descend;
then in a flurry of flapping feathers,
screeching fearful guffaws
swoop and stretch
uncanny strings of gut
stuffing craws
with rotting carrion;
yet soon to soar again
quite out of sight
oblivious to our plight.

There was no point now in not telling him where I came from. I told him I was from British Guiana. His face lit up. Unbelievably he had been there!

I recalled that as a very small boy a German Moravian minister had stayed with my family. My father had himself been a Moravian Minister. Our guest had been a charming soft-spoken man who had served in the trenches during the First World War. He had told me the story of how his bible had saved his life. He always kept it on his person, in his breast-pocket, and it had stopped a piece of shrapnel entering his chest!

We talked about Guiana in very general terms. I cannot remember what he had done there, but thereafter the Commanding Officer always saluted me whenever we chanced to meet on his rounds around the camp.

The camp was divided into six compounds, each holding approximately 1,000 prisoners. The centre compound, where I was to spend my first six months of captivity, was about 200 yards long and 75 yards wide. There were about ten barrack blocks, each holding one hundred prisoners. Each block was again subdivided into ten 'messes', with ten prisoners to each mess. A mess was equivalent to a family, of sorts, within our POW community.

In my mess were Vern White and Jerry Houston, both Canadian Officers who were with me throughout our captivity. Jerry became my *mucker*, the guy who shared mess duties with me on a rota basis. We have been in touch ever since until his death a few years ago. I am still in touch with Vern whose unpublished memoir has acted as an aid memoir for sections of this chapter in our lives together. Another member was Max Ellis a much older man, an air gunner on a pathfinder Squadron. He had once been a soldier of fortune, having served five years with the French Foreign Legion. He had also attended Sandhurst Military College where apparently, one of his classmates was David Niven. He was a very reticent man but we were all very intrigued by him. Max had succeeded in escaping from the camp by concealing himself under a horse drawn wagon and making it into the countryside, sleeping in a deserted barn when he needed to rest, only to be awakened by the sound of barking dogs and of German soldiers milling around. Poor Max, he had escaped on the very night that the Great Escape from the Centre Compound had taken place! He was captured and brought back to camp. I remember running into him years after the war in the Kings Road, Chelsea, but the difference in our ages was a barrier to us getting close.

Each week a new consignment of POWs arrived, some of whom joined our mess, staying together when we were eventually moved to Belaria, a smaller camp for British Officers five kilometres away. We would all flock to the perimeter-fence to welcome them. We each hoped that other members of our respective crews would show up.

Four other members of my crew were officers. I knew that one had been killed but I was always on the lookout for the arrival of one or other of the three unaccounted for. Each time I had gone down to join the reception committee I had been disappointed, but one day I thought I saw a figure that vaguely reminded me of Al, my pilot. Surely that could not be him!

There was no sign of either of my other crewmembers, but I waited to greet the new arrivals as they entered the main gate. As they flooded through, amidst our cynical greetings, one of them separated himself from the rest and came towards me. Could this piteous looking specimen, after all, be Al? He sported a heavy beard and his head was leaning heavily to one side, but the voice was unmistakable.

"Hi Cy," he greeted me, "how did the *tatoes* turn out!"

Al never lost his sense of humour.

"Al!", I blurted out. "Man, whatever happened to your neck! A great improvement, I must confess!"

I was bursting with happiness and joy, yet there I was, trying to match his jokes. Al was probably the only person who could have broken his neck and survived! His head was to remain listing to one side forever. But to have him with me in the same camp was the best thing that had happened to me since I had been shot down.

Al was the most charismatic person I've known: warm, witty, cheerful – a born leader of men. Even in his weakened state he took charge. He formed his own mess, just as he had chosen his crew. There were twelve of us – ten Canadians, an Irishman and myself.

We had the cleanest, best-organised mess. Al could do anything with his hands. At first we had no pots and pans, but in the end we had cups and plates. He even built a radio that worked from scraps he scrounged from other prisoners and from the German guards, who were not averse to a bit of bribery. After all, we had much more than they had, the Red Cross saw to that. We even ate better than the German guards as we received food parcels from the Red Cross. Although sometimes they were held up, most of us received one parcel every week. They came from England, the USA and Canada. As ours was a mostly Canadian mess we looked forward to receiving the Canadian ones, which contained corned beef, salmon, sardines, jam or marmalade, powdered milk, prunes, sugar, tea or coffee, cheese, biscuits, chocolate, in small amounts and cigarettes. We could trade cigarettes with the German guards and so were able to build radios. We created a community which was self-sufficient and was run with military precision. All we missed was our freedom – and of course, women.

Over a very short period of time our prisoner-of-war community organized itself into an orderly and highly functioning unit. Within each mess, each individual played his part in contributing to the welfare of the camp as a whole, whilst the Senior British Officer was responsible for general discipline and ensured that the Camp Commandant adhered to the rights of prisoners of war under the Geneva Convention. He was uncompromising in demanding that these were strictly observed. We received parcels of food from the International Red Cross on a fairly regular basis and in general life in the camp was extremely well organized.

Apart from the daily *apels,* one in the morning and the other in the evening, the Germans left us more-or-less to our own devices. They were, of course, continuously snooping to check up on any tunnelling.

~ A Member of the RAF of Indeterminate Race ~

Prisoner-of-war camps are not concentration camps and as far as I know no one was tortured. We were not made to work, being officers, and we were not ill-treated. But what comforts we enjoyed were due chiefly to our own efforts, as well as to the Red Cross. For me being a prisoner of war for 2 years was equivalent to having a University education. Not only did I have an opportunity to reflect upon my life, about who I was, what I was doing there and what had brought me into that situation, but I was in the company of men who were officers, well educated and above average intelligence. We were able to organize ourselves into a highly efficient community - Escape committees, recreation facilities, libraries, theatre groups, a jazz band, (in which I played) and music societies. I actually ran a music society for my block and in so doing increased my own knowledge of European classical music. I had played piano as a boy, my mother being a music teacher. We also had a few reference books and a small collection of records.

The first few months of captivity were the hardest, for until a camp is properly organized it can be quite a daunting environment. There was no access to reliable news about the progress of the war, only the occasional letter from home (heavily censored). There was also a shortage of decent food and the uncomfortable two-tiered wooden beds. Uncertainty about the outcome of the war did not help the situation.

Incarceration was a period for deep reflection upon the fact that if one had not been shot down, one would be still be on operations. We were all well aware that only a small minority of aircrews finished their first tour.

I was to learn later that the period 1943-44 marked the most intensive bombing of Germany by the Allies, with an estimated loss of 19,000 aircrew lives This represented only a one in four chance of survival during the period. The total loss of aircrew for the entire war was an estimated 47,000 lives, with a further 10,000 as prisoners of war – out of an estimated total of 125,000 aircrew who flew in the war. In a very sobering sense we were lucky to be alive and awaiting the end of hostilities.

Doubt

When I am rent with doubt
that all I see about and strive to write of
is not beheld by thee
that all the tears of love
and humanity to you are naught
then am I distraught

And if I know that all I sing
is but a tuneless dirge
a mockery that could not bring
but me delight, some worthless thing devoid of poetry,
then since there be such overwhelming urge
I to myself alone shall sing.

During this time I actually began to question how I got to be in this situation and to look back at my life in Guyana and what had prompted me to join up. It certainly had nothing to do with patriotism and although I had not been subject to racism in any form in the services, I was well aware that racism was part-and-parcel of colonialism and therefore part of my life experience.

I had been born into a system which prescribed an English education, a Eurocentric version of history and a language which denied me an authentic identity. It had made me feel inadequate in so many inexplicable ways. It had cast a shadow over my inner being. Later I would question all the values of this *civilization* – including its notions of justice and fair play on which I had been nurtured.

But at that time, the centre of the world remained firmly in Europe. It was only later that I learned about other cultures, about the true history of Egypt and Africa as a whole; of the spirituality of the East, of the genius of China; of the similarity of Copernicus' heliocentric system to the Aztec calendar; that Muslim, Chinese and Egyptian astronomers preceded Galileo and Copernicus; that the ancient Dogon of Africa knew about the existence of Sirius B long before the West, and of so much more besides...

But even before I was to learn all these things, I had never felt inferior as a human being to any other person. True, I was aware that white people always presumed that they were somehow intrinsically superior, but my experience in the colonies and in England never confirmed such a view.

I passed the time by keeping a log, reading, playing the guitar in the band, and playing games – hockey and volley-ball. I had played hockey for my county in British Guiana. I also was in great demand to make portraits of girlfriends of prisoners – enlargements of photographs.

I had always been good at this. My father had recognized this talent when he had me 'blow-up' that picture of Toussaint L'Overture of Haiti for him. I did not realize then that he had been educating me. Little was I to know then what a symbolic figure Toussaint would be for me in later life.

I always had it in mind that if I survived the war I would study law. The law seemed the best career for those who had political aspirations. Politics per se did not interest me, but I saw it as a possible weapon against colonialism.

There were no other black officers in the Camp. As yet there was no obvious racism directed towards me, and per-haps because I was in a predominantly Canadian ('colonial') mess with Al, my pilot, being particularly popular and sought after, I basked in that popularity too. There was only one occasion I remember when an American airman called me a nigger! He was from the deep South, I gathered, and just could not understand that I was an officer in the British Air Force.

The Move to Belaria

After a stay of approximately six months at Stalag Luft 3, the majority of British officers from the centre compound were moved to a smaller officers' camp, known as Belaria, about five kilometres south. We were to remain there until the end of January 1945.

We soon became a settled community of seasoned *kriegies* with the growing sense of individual freedom to pursue our own interests. Many and varied activities sprang into being. Soon we had music societies, a concert orchestra and dance band led by Len Whitely. I played in this band having been taught a few modern jazz chords by an American prisoner at Stalag 3 who had played in the Glen Miller Orchestra. There was also organized sport, newspapers – The 'Log' and 'Gefangener Gazette', which carried cartoons of prison life, poems, articles and editorials and which were proudly displayed on reserved wall space; home made radios with which to follow the progress of the war, a library and Reference Library. I was made responsible for a music club and discovered classical music. I had listened to classical music all my life and had studied piano. My mother was a piano teacher and most of my sisters played the instrument but I never really appreciated the Classics until I had to run the club. I also read a lot. An English ex-Head Master, Charlie Russell, was my literary guide. He was an unusually cultivated and unprejudiced English gentleman.

In time, too, we had a theatre. The sets were excellent and the costumes were often as good as we were able to hire them from Berlin for our period-plays. Those cast as girls, though not exactly fetching, reminded us of what we were missing in our lives other than the freedom to come and go as we pleased. But probably the most important of the organizations was the escape committee which had its own underground intelligence. It employed tailors, professors, draughtsman, architects, electrical engineers, detectives, forgers and even ordinary stooges like myself.

Every prisoner of war had the duty to try to escape or assist in the escape of other prisoners and so was part of the vast escape organisation, even though most were never destined to get out and make a bid for liberty.

The Germans countered with their ferrets or guards with their dogs, their searchlights which incessantly swept the camp at night, and their rolls of barbed wire. There vas an unrelenting struggle to outwit each other and although the Germans certainly held most of the cards we constantly outsmarted them.

Our surveillance network was quite sophisticated. Each German ferret was named in such a manner that no one could possibly mistake him. Such names as 'Popeye', 'Hatchet-Face' and 'Slim'. The one exception was Hans, who never qualified for a name because he was quite young and inoffensive. He had lost his toes on the Eastern Front and did not appreciate his posting as a prison guard! Some prisoners were constantly employed to watch each of the entrances into the camp, and the time of arrival and departure of each ferret was logged, until after a time it was reasonably easy to know how and where they were disposed over the camp.

The ferrets were even encouraged to form habits – bad habits for ferrets. Their job was not an enviable one. They came into daily contact with the prisoners and it was only natural that they tried to make their own lives bearable by wanting to appear friendly. After all, we had the chocolate the cigarettes and the spare time. In a strange sense, we were also – in view of our relaxed discipline and organisation – the privileged ones.

Hans was our assignment. Every other prisoner completely ignored him, but in our mess he was made to feel like a human being. As time went by he gravitated more and more towards our barrack block. He accepted our cups of tea and soon felt so at home with us that he often outstayed his welcome, even after the need for the decoy was no longer necessary.

Tunnelling was almost always in progress. In some cases two or even three were being dug at the same time. Whenever the Germans found out about a tunnel they never intervened until the very last moment, for in this way they knew that we were harmlessly occupied. For our part, tunnels were evacuated for the sole purpose of being so discovered while other more serious operations were in progress elsewhere. The Germans often fell into the traps that were so cunningly laid for them; it was usually too late when they finally decided the time had come to intervene and close down the dummy tunnels. And so the battle of wits continued to the very end.

During my overall period of captivity few prisoners actually escaped. Attempts by small groups were always being made, but most ended in recapture. The remarkable breakout, known as the 'Wooden Horse' [exemplifying the Trojan legend], took place on 29th October 1943 from the east compound of my original camp, Sagan. But a massive outbreak, 'the Great Escape', took place a year later, on 24th March 1944 from the north compound at Sagan. The superb organisation that made it possible exemplifies, above all else, the patient determination and undaunted spirit of the majority of prisoners. The tunnel was perfectly constructed and even had electric lighting. All this under the very noses of the German guards and their dogs!

Weeks later came the news that forty prisoners had been recaptured and shot. This figure was later confirmed as fifty. This news sent a wave of resentment and bitterness towards the Germans that never left us. Loud protestations were made by the Senior British Officer and a policy of non-cooperation came into effect. From henceforth we were as awkward as we possibly could be.

On Thursday, 13 April, a memorial service was held immediately after the morning apels on the sports ground. It took the form of a parade service. I cannot recall any parade, in captivity or out, which was executed with more solemnity and precision. Even thinking about it now is quite moving.

I was to learn later that a memorial service was also held in London's St Martin-in-the-Fields Chapel for these officers. There was also a memorial service on December 4th at Stalag Luft III cemetery. This Service was attended by the Swiss Minister to Germany and officers from all nationalities. A memorial with three tablets engraved with the names of all the officers killed was erected.

In many ways Thursday 13 April 1944 epitomized both the spirit of prisoners-of-war and our frustrations, for on that very day the Germans perpetrated a heartless stunt as preposterous as it was callous. As we were dispersing from the service, deeply moved as we were, we were halted completely in our tracks. Suddenly a loud shout went up. A moment's hesitation before we caught on that something exceptional was taking place at the main gate to the camp.

We all surged forward excitedly, hearts pounding, throats screaming hoarsely in hope. There, on the other side of the gate, the focus of all our dreams for so long – British soldiers! – a private first, with a sergeant behind him. Then other soldiers, bayonets drawn, our captive guards between them!

It was not until having run to the entrance that the sergeant turned threateningly towards us, gun in hand, bellowing *"Inter barraken!"*

The uniforms were so perfect. Our hopes so tangible.

In the background a movie camera was panning the scene, recording our protests as a 'British' soldier prodded with the butt of his rifle the head of a German soldier already heavily swathed in bandages.

What a diabolical hoax! We were 'German' prisoners in a 'British' POW camp! The Goebbels propaganda machine was fabricating evidence of 'British atrocities'.

Wan Cynthia! How sadly sits your throne!
How still the night! How spectral white your face!
Your listless footsteps trail in anguished pace
the clouds that are from Winter's bosom blown.
Is it for sorrow for some youth unknown
that fell unlimbered from the hostile skies?
Is it for pity that he unsung lies
in some secluded field o'er which he'd flown
just one short minute past? Or is it still
the writhing throes of sad Europa's toils
that blanch thee, like the year's last daffodil?
Bemoan no more. O moon, these ills, these spoils
or think not that these ravages can kill
the Peace god's son, though pierced by five years' foils

4. The March[11]

Last week sleigh bells jangled along this road;
Now babies cry and old hags die.

We followed the course of the war with mounting excitement throughout the rest of the year. We plotted the advances of the British and American forces from the West and that of the Russians from the East. Prisoners-of- war were una-bashed optimists. They were always prepared to wager that the war would be over in the next six months. Long enough to maintain reasonable hope but not too long a period to en-dure. As the Allied forces advanced this period became shorter and shorter.

By January 1945, the chances of being liberated did seem very good indeed. The maps all indicated that both the Americans and the Russians armies were closing fast. There were bets as to which one would get to us first. But it was chiefly to the East that we looked for our salvation. The Rus-sians were sweeping everything before them in a colossal drive commencing in January 1945. The first visible signs of the proximity of the war came with the first bedraggled col-

---

[11] Not to be confused with 'The Long March' endured by other prisoners of war from Poland to Germany, in harrowing and severe winter conditions, from January to April 1945, a memorial to which can be viewed at the R.A.F Museum, Hendon. For details of this see *Of Ploughs, Planes and Palliasses* by Percy Wilson Carruthers (Woodfield, 1992) or *From Fiji to Balkan Skies* (Woodfield, 2000).

umns of the retreating German Army. And after they had passed along the road that ran adjacent to our Camp on the top of the hill the refugees started to go by. A tiny trickle at first, but within the next two days their numbers had swollen to a long never-ending pilgrimage of misery and suffering – oxen-drawn carts and creaking wagons laden with the entire effects of families, the old and the very young plodding their weary souls over the frozen ground in a gloomy procession.

To us prisoners though, this misery was the prelude to our own liberation. The Russians could not get to us fast enough. We huddled around our maps, laid wagers, made calculations; at this rate we would be free men next Tuesday! Next Tuesday! Our minds could hardly cope with the excitement and all the possibilities that were suddenly opening up for us! Then at 9.30 on the night of January 27, when the stage seemed set, the bomb exploded. No, we were not blown to bits, only our dreams, our cherished dreams which had kept us going for the greater part of two years. We were told to be ready to be evacuated in thirty minutes. Panic! Thirty minutes! We were to be moved westwards, away from the advancing Russians.

Dejection, like a grim vulture, hovered over the camp. Fear crept into our hearts. We were without large reserves of food. The next Red Cross parcels were expected the following day. There had been very heavy snow falls all month and the landscape was a sea of glistening white; the Germans would be hostile in the towns as well as in the villages; we may be caught between the two armies...

But, notwithstanding all these considerations, we drew comfort from the realisation that the Germans were being defeated, that the war was coming to an end and our destiny would be resolved sooner rather than later. The long wait was almost over.

It was shortly after midnight before we were told to assemble for departure. Then, after hanging about for over an hour and a half, we were told that the start was going to be further delayed. This was a welcome respite and we seized the opportunity to check again on what we would be taking with us – the bare essentials.

We eventually set out at about 8 am on the morning of Sunday 28 January, having each collected a whole Red Cross food parcel. Along with American POW's there were more than a thousand of us, heading we knew not where. Therein started a battle against uncertainly, fear and the elements. We were being moved in the wrong direction. The Russians were only 45 kilometres (28 miles, approximately) away at Steinau. The weather was below freezing and everything was covered in thick snow. Were we strong enough to survive a rigorous trek, probably lasting several days?

As a group, our mess of twelve had taken the decision to stick together and pool our resources. Our hurriedly made sledge just held our bare necessities. Ours was the biggest on the snow and it proved a great boon. Once under way it moved along more easily than the smaller ones and we took it in turns pulling it, three shifts of four men, each for a period of 20 minutes, so none of us had to carry a rucksack.

~ A Member of the RAF of Indeterminate Race ~

That first day was a nightmare. We got so tired that it would have been a relief to simply collapse onto the snow. But no one collapsed on the first day. We stopped only twice, just long enough to eat something. To stand still for longer than five minutes would have been to invite disaster, for the cold was intense and the risk of frostbite very great; it was better to keep moving, and this we did, on frozen feet, all day long.

Trudging along a road which ran adjacent to a dense wood, we saw some German Storm Troopers dressed in their white winter uniforms. These were the *creme-de-la-creme* of the German Army; big, healthy-looking men, looking quite magnificent. They were deployed in the wood and took no notice of us straggling along in the snow. I looked at them apprehensively. They were fine specimens of Hitler's so-called *master race* alright, but you sensed that fate was catching up with them fast.

When we eventually arrived at Kunau, at 5.30 pm, we had covered 20 kilometres (12 miles). It was quite dark as we scrambled to make our beds in the huge communal barn of the village. The barn was absolutely pitch black and the climb into the clean hay in the loft strenuous, to say the least. I shall never forget the stampede as 1,000 prisoners vied with each other to find a comfortable corner in which to pass the night. I slept little that night, and neither did many of us. I never really got warm, even though I buried myself deep down into the straw, the dust from which filled my eyes and throat. The lucky ones were those who did not get into the loft but who managed to get a cow to sleep with! 'Warm and friendly,' they pronounced the next day.

The dawn of January 29 was greeted with great apprehension by most of us. It was cold and grey, the sunshine as weak as our starved spirits. But by eight o'clock we were under way again and trudged through Wiesau towards Gross Selten. The German people along the way were generally friendly and gave us hot water, bread and other things in exchange for cigarettes, which we had in abundance. The guards themselves were not enjoying the long march, most of them being fairly old, and did not object to this fraternizing, but the Luftwaffe officers in charge of the columns vainly tried to stop it.

We arrived at Gross Selten at about 4 pm, having covered another 20 kilometres, but the going had been easier and our spirits were consequently much lighter. There was plenty of scrap wood about the farmyard and we were able to make hot meals of corned beef and whatever we had before settling down in a barn. It had electric lights, so we were able to see where we were and could contrive to make ourselves much more comfortable than we had been on the previous night.

We were awakened the following morning to the good news that we would not be moved that day. This was very welcome, but with time on our hands the inevitable rumour machine began to operate... we had lost contact with High Command, the guards were without specific orders, we were stranded somewhere between the two armies, the Russians were only a few kilometres away... The uncertainty prompted some prisoners to take off on their own and chance their luck.

During the day, part of a German Panzer Division arrived, retreating from the Russians. It consisted of several lorries, overcrowded with soldiers, and an officer in his car. Surprisingly, they were very friendly towards us. They sensed that they had 'had it' and that it might be in their interests to have some friends. They swapped their rations for coffee and cigarettes and said that the war could be over in a couple of days. This cheered us up immensely. We built several small fires to brew-up and keep warm and a relaxed atmosphere prevailed.

But this did not last long. The German Officer discovered that the goose he had commandeered and which he had left in his car, had vanished into thin air. He made a great fuss and made threatening noises. But it was too late. His goose had not only been cooked but had disappeared into the hungry bellies of some enterprising British prisoners-of-war! Goosezumped! He settled for a bar of chocolate and some American cigarettes.

The following day, January 30, after a complete rest and general overhaul, we were up and marching by 8 am. The going was easier now. We passed through Tappferstadt and by 2pm we had arrived at Birkenstadt. We had covered another 21 kilometres. We camped in the communal barn there. The weather was much warmer and we spent a comfortable night there after being locked in the barn at 5 pm.

We awoke the next day to find that a miracle had happened overnight. A great thaw was in progress, induced by torrential overnight rainfall. It was rapidly transforming everything into a lake of slush and surging muddy water. We were not moved that day because it was said that the groups ahead of us had slowed down and there was no accommodation ahead for us. This was just as well, as the roads would have been slippery and treacherous with the thaw.

It was a miserable day, hanging around in the slush, wet underfoot with mud and straw sticking to one's soaking boots. The knowledge that we would have to abandon our sledges and carry our packs on our backs did not help.

We received our first German rations since setting out five days before – a fifth of a loaf of bread each. The owner of the farm where we were billeted complained bitterly when we moved the straw to make ourselves comfortable. We were, in turn, quite unmoved, threatening to report him to the Geneva Convention for mistreatment of British Officers!

February 2 was even more miserable than the first day we set out. Hunger was beginning to have its effect, for up to that point we had only received one hot meal – a bowl of soup and a fifth of a loaf of bread. The going was tough. Now there were stragglers and men collapsed onto the banks of sludge by the side of the river of mud through which we waded ankle deep. Many would have been left behind had it not been for the heroic and strenuous work of our untiring Medical Officer, who, equipped with an oxcart, rescued the fallen and tended the sick.

By the time we arrived at Schonheide, a small village on the outskirts of Spremberg, we were practically in a state of collapse. We were split up into groups of about 100 men each and for the first time marched off to dispersed barns for the night. My group were put into a damp, straw-less, unlit barn and the doors bolted. After munching biscuits lightly spread with margarine we settled down to get some sleep. We were dead beat.

We woke next morning, February 3, stiff and aching and marched into Spremberg. We were taken to a tank corps depot and locked into the empty shed. We were treated to a bowl of very thick soup, our first real hot meal in 7 days. We were then marched to the railway station and at about 4.30 herded into box cars, 46 men to each car – approximately 24ft by 8ft. We were so cramped that we had to take it in turns to lie or sit down. It was not until some five hours later that the train began to move, taking us on the last stage of our journey. We had walked some 95 kms in seven days. Now we were being taken like cattle, we knew not whither.

Next morning we were still moving. The train had made several stops during the night. In the congested space, none of us managed any sleep and the frequent stops were alarming. The journey was interrupted several times during the following day and we peered through the slats only to see sidings and desolate surroundings. We arrived at Lukenwalde at 17.00 hours precisely.

It was just getting dark and the Germans counted and recounted us for what seemed hours before marching us off. It started to rain. It took one and a half hours standing outside the gates before we were allowed to enter the camp, where we were to remain until the end of the war.

5. Stalag 3a, Lukenwalde[12]

That these our days of youth are barren spent
in idleness, and void of nature's wonderment,
lacking the zest for life,
ascribed the fickle jest of destiny,
embittered by the strife
deluded by a sad reality.

That these our days of youth should pass
that hope should wither as the sun-scorched grass
that all be thought as naught
or else be fraught with fears
then time it is for tears.

We entered the camp at 8 pm but it was not until 6 am the following morning that we were finally shown into our barracks. In took all night to search and delouse us! Why they bothered to do so escaped us, for the barracks were squalid and dirty, with broken windows and damp walls. They had previously been occupied by Russian prisoners, who must have been moved to one of the other compounds. There were no stoves and the water had either been turned off or the pipes were frozen. The filthy palliasses on the three-tiered bunks were lumpy and over run with bedbugs. Each room

---

[12] A Stalag was where POWs from every branch of the services were held, and by this time included more than a dozen different nationalities. Stalag Lufts, where we were previously held, were for aircrew only.

contained twelve bunks and within half an hour of entering the rooms we were filthier than when we had arrived. We began to itch before even crawling into the bunks.

Lukenwalde was a huge POW camp, 50 kilometres south of Berlin. It was divided into several compounds, *Stalags* and *Oflags*, housing many nationalities, American, Russian, French, Yugoslav, Norwegian, Czechoslovakian and British – in all about 25,000 officers and men. We were the only Royal Air Force personnel and our Group Captain was the senior British Officer. There was a large section where captured American GIs camped out in huge tents.

Life here, in the closing months of the war, was beastly. There was little to eat. No longer recipients of Red Cross parcels, we now had to subsist on the meagre rations provided by the Germans – one-fifth of a loaf of bread, an ounce of margarine, six potatoes, and a bowl of soup *per diem*. At noon there was the familiar sight of four prisoners carrying a huge container of soup, with a pole under the handles. The soup was made from worm-infested peas and horsemeat, but we just scooped out the worms and wolfed it down. All we thought about was food, and we planned gourmet feasts in our imagination for the day we were finally back home! Cigarettes were now practically non-existent and of course there was no longer any mail to look forward to. But worst of all, there were no books. I realized how much I had depended on the library at Belaria.

Added to this, it was bitterly cold, so in spite of the bed bugs we clung to our miserable bunks for most of the day. The blankets were so scanty that if there was any warmth generated it was from the continuous scratching engendered by our constant itching. At night, sleep was almost impossible, because of the activity of our bed companions. When we did manage to drop off, fear stalked our dreams.

the world revolves
but time stands still;
distant memories:
laughter, hurry John we'll miss the fun
Desiree, you are so soft, I love you;
the city clock booming the hour
hurrying faces, kiosks... a stranger's smile
What's the matter, son?
I slipped on barbed wire, Dad
'Barberd wire?' Let me see,
there, its not too bad
it will not hurt within the hour..

the world revolving
time standing still....

there's an awful stench in this room.
On three-tiered bunks we lie
prisoners
staring with vacant eye.

The German guards were jittery and consequently very harsh. There was no access to German newspapers and it was some time before we were able to put together a wireless to get dependable news about the progress of the war. Our spirits lifted considerably after we received a gift of Danish Red Cross parcels from fellow Norwegian Officers. This was a few weeks after we had arrived in the camp.

In mid-March, the first American Red Cross parcels arrived, and soon we were taking control of our living quarters. We realized how important it was to maintain morale and discipline and to negotiate with the Germans for our supplies of food, water and electricity. Our success varied with the circumstances, the ambivalence of the Germans and their own expectations; sometimes wanting to keep in our good books, but at other times resentful of the way things were going for Germany.

Then on April 9, a rumour started spreading in the camp. We were to be moved yet again to a place called Moosburg, near Munich. The next day this was officially confirmed.

To pass the time, I decided to continue with my record. Would I be able to sort out the collection of notes made on scraps of paper and in pencil when it was all over? I felt beleaguered and bombarded by a legion of suppressed desires and unresolved mental conflicts – desire for freedom of action, from crowded confined spaces, to be clean, for decent food, for home-life, friends and female companionship.

Nearly two years of imprisonment had given me the opportunity to reconsider my life and re-assess my decision to join the Royal Air Force. Was I fighting for King and Country? Or was my fight to escape the life inherited by being born on the wrong side of the British colonial system? Was Hitler's thirst for empire any different from that of the Europe of the last three hundred years? Already the super powers were carving up Eastern Europe, just as they had carved up Africa in the last century.

Rumours had also been reaching us about the gas chamber atrocities perpetrated by the Germans on the Jews of Europe. This barbarism was being carried out by Europeans. In the past, European versions of history had somehow always justified their own barbarities. How would they explain this away? How was this latest barbarism different from that of the Middle Passage and the institution of slavery? What was the difference, if any, between claims of racial superiority as an aesthetic and as justification for exploitation for profit? As yet, these questions were still unresolved, but they continued to simmer in the back of my consciousness. They were to remain central to my life and to my efforts to reconcile my experience as a black man with an understanding of the deeper philosophical realities which somehow were in revolt against the European spirit of domination of man and nature.

Standing by to move to some other desolate POW camp was torture. Despite the filthy, overcrowded conditions and the drab monotony of our existence at Lukenwalde, we dreaded this move. The disrupted state of the German railroads, the refugee-ridden roads, the heavily-bombed communications, the shortage of food and the possibility that we may be strafed by our own air force, filled us with foreboding.

What was the point of it all? Where could they take us this time? The Allies were advancing on all fronts and fast. The western front formed a line approximately stretching from

Bremen in the north to Hanover, Celle Gotha, east of Wurtsburg, Stuttgart and a few miles southwest of Nuremberg. On the eastern front, the Russians were massed along the River Oder from Stettin, south of Frankfurt, along the Niesse to the Gorlitz area, curving to the east south of Breslau, Czechoslovakia to Vienna in Austria. They had started an offensive in the Gorlitz area, driving towards Dresden.

Later that day, a few German officers came to see the British Commanding Officer. This, we thought, meant that we were about to set out. Then came a second announcement. Two senior officers, along with an interpreter, had been taken away. No reason was given, but we presumed that they were to precede us in order to make plans for our arrival at Moosburg.

"Stand by to move within the next twelve hours." Came the order, and shortly afterwards another notice: "Parade in full marching order at 10.30am tomorrow, the 12th, on the sports field.

So we would be moving after all! The suspense we had felt during the last days of January, which had preceded the march, was back with us. But it was worse this time.

We left the barracks at approximately 11am and marched to the same railway station at which we had arrived just two months earlier. Here, again, we were made to hang around for hours. We were, of course, acutely aware of the danger of going anywhere by rail and some officers persuaded the Germans to give us sufficient yellow paint to daub 'R.A.F – P.O.W.' in huge letters of the top of the carriages. During this period we each received about half a litre of pea soup. Later, with nothing much to do, I passed the time observing the Germans, who hung around, collecting our cigarette butts. What a droll lot!

One remarkable thing about the country was the large number of small children to be seen everywhere. At noon a German civilian slapped a small boy for volunteering to fetch some water for one of the prisoners. He screamed at him "*English! English!*" as though the prisoner had the plague. But I knew that deep down they would welcome the arrival of the British or American forces instead of the Russians. When his back was turned, the kids were back, having the time of their lives, playing with the *krieges*, not in the least afraid of the English.

And so the afternoon dragged on. I decided to read a book which had been going the rounds (I do not recall its name and made no note of it). Then at around 6pm we were made to enter the boxcars. Again we were crowded together, but this time we made an effort to organise ourselves better for the very long journey we expected. Forty to each boxcar, this time, was marginally better than on the last occasion. Somehow we got news that the Allies were at Stendal, about 100 km west of Berlin.

We lay on our sides, jammed like sardines hard against one another in two rows, facing each other with feet interlocking. The atmosphere was stifling and it was impossible to sleep. This seemed a great hardship, until I recalled the purgatory endured by slaves, my forebears, of the Middle Passage, a journey of some six thousand miles. What was one night cramped like sardines in a cold boxcar, compared to weeks drowning in despair, violence, vomit and excreta in the holds of a slave ship? I lay awake most of that night in the utter darkness of the boxcar, praying that we would not be strafed by the RAF.

Dawn broke the next day, Friday 13 April, dismal and cold. We were all terribly cramped and could hardly move, but were allowed to scramble out of the boxcars. We each received a Red Cross food parcel, about 4 lbs of tinned food. How long it was supposed to last, we had no idea, but we would be digging into it sparingly. We had hardly received anything from the Red Cross in the last weeks. We also received an eighth of a loaf of bread, our daily ration, with a spoonful of margarine.

We had not moved. The engine that was to pull the train had not turned up. The staff at the railway station somehow doubted that it would. It was perfect weather for the RAF and much too hot to be in the boxcars. We were allowed to camp outside the railway station.

The German civilians living nearby were very friendly. There was news that the Allies had crossed the Elbe and were within 56 miles of Berlin and 12 miles of Halle.

Later on, a locomotive came into view, but went right past us and disappeared round a bend. If it was intended to pull us, it would have to switch tracks and sidle up to where we were waiting. We were never to be sure, for shortly afterwards, at approximately 1.45pm, two American Thunderbolts flew low overhead in the same direction. Soon there was the sound of cannon fire and a loud explosion, followed by a huge erupting cloud of steam...

Was this providence? For us it was.

The evacuation was abandoned the next day. There had been no further sighting of a locomotive, so we were made to march back to the camp to a deafening reception by the prisoners who had been left behind.

The attitude of the Germans had changed dramatically. They became polite and positively obsequious, some asking for good conduct notes! They were hoping that the British or Americans would get there before the Russians.

That night there was a spectacular air raid on Potsdam. The night sky was ablaze and the muffled sound of the bombardment could be heard even though we were miles away. Then came the news confirming that the Americans had crossed the Elbe south of Magdeburg and had established a bridgehead about 40 miles away from the camp.

Even if an engine had turned up to move us, there would have been nowhere to go.

On the 15th, the day after our return to camp, there was an identification check at 3pm. The following day the Russian offensive began on the eastern front, the Oder-Neisse line. By the 17th we were looking to the west, to the south and to the east. Flares and flashes were seen on the horizon at night. On the 18th big fires were observed to the west. We could hear gunfire in the distance. The excitement was mounting with each passing day.

At midnight the following day came the order, "Stand by to move" (again!), but the following afternoon, Marauder fighters flew directly overhead and Juterborg (Jüterbog) was bombed. It lay only a few miles south of our position. The next day, April 20, the Russians were at Juterborg and the Germans were looking very anxious. They would shortly be leaving us to our fate. Large scale air raids continued for most of the day.

At about 1 am on the morning of Sunday 21 April, a German aircraft strafed the camp. We bailed out of our beds in great panic and huddled on the floor. But it was just one random pass over the main road through the camp and his shells did no damage. This incident must have scared even the German guards, for later that day, at about 11am, we began to feel that a change had come over the camp.

At first we were not sure what it was, until someone pointed out that the sentry boxes were no longer manned. By midday the Germans started gathering just outside the main gates.

The senior POW officer was sent for, but when he was not immediately found they handed over the camp to the most senior officer they could find, an American, before taking off. Shortly afterwards the camp came under the control of the Norwegian General, Otto Rude, who was the most senior officer in the camp.

With the war coming swiftly to a close, it became necessary for the official POW Defense Scheme, which had been decided in advance, to come into effect. This entailed keeping the vital services of the camp intact, liaising with the other nationalities for our mutual welfare and patrolling the perimeter to discourage prisoners from trying to leave on their own.

~ A Member of the RAF of Indeterminate Race ~

On the very day the Germans departed, I was enlisted as a member of a small search party, which looted the Truppen-lager. The Germans had left everything behind: radios, food, drink, official documents and photographs and a few luxuries. Each mess was provided with a radio, champagne, and a few eggs!

The following are extracts from the British Intelligence summary:

> In the woods near the Lararette, there is a party of Germans consisting of seven or eight SS Troops and 100 other soldiers. They have visited the Lazarette and state that anyone outside the camp after dark will be fired upon and reprisals will be made for any overt acts of hostility. The German General commanding light artillery threatened to open fire on the camp unless 8 rifles taken from his men were found and returned.
>
> The rifles were handed over.
>
> At 9 o'clock, it was reported that only about 1,000 Volksturm and Hitler Youth armed with tommy-guns and panzer-fausts were defending Lukenwalde. Several buildings and factories were ablaze in the town, which was bombed by Russian aircraft this afternoon.

April 22 (Extract continued):

> At 00.30 hrs, a delegation from the ex-Mayor of Lukenwalde visited the camp and offered to hand the town over to the camp authorities for subsequent surrender to the Russian Army. The delegation stated that

the Volksturm units in the town had been disbanded and that there were no Germans troops left there.

At 01.15 hrs, 9 Germans soldiers moving N.W. past the camp reported that the line was 2-3 miles S.E and 4 miles N.E of Lukenwalde.

At 06.00 hrs, the first Russian armoured car entered the camp and left half an hour later, taking General Rude, the Senior Allied Officer, to Lukenwalde. Owing to being fired upon near the camp, the Senior American Officer and an interpreter, who were riding on an armoured car (actually they were hanging on to the side of the same armoured car) ended their journey rapidly; returning to the camp on foot while the armoured car proceeded to Lukenwalde.

At: 08.15 hrs, Russian infantry were seen from the Norwegian Compound advancing into the woods west of the camp.

At 10 am the same day, 22nd April, six tanks and 29 motorized units carrying Russian soldiers crashed through the camp, literally tearing down the perimeter fence amidst our cheers and excitement. This was the day we were waiting for, the day we had been anticipating for some time now. At last we were liberated. Soon we'd be back in Britain, alive and able to start our lives again. Words cannot describe the scene! Our liberators were war scarred fighting soldiers, a few women amongst them, flushed, wild-looking and armed to the teeth. Some had distinctly Mongolian features. We crowded around their tanks, cheering in joy and disbelief, taken aback by the magnitude of the moment – feeling the barbarism of war oozing from their bodies, their eyes, their entire demeanour. Free at last!

Some Russian prisoners, who were strong enough, clambered aboard the tanks and were soon heading in the direction of Berlin.

A German group in the woods to the west of the camp opened fire with machine guns, but caused no casualties.

A new chapter had opened in our lives and the question uppermost in our minds was, 'How long before we get back to Blighty?'

6. The Plight of the Eagles

Throughout that day, we were to hear sporadic bursts of machine gun fire from the woods bordering the camp as Russian troops mopped up. The battle moved to the north-east, to the north- west and west of the camp. The town of Lukenwalde was occupied and in the camps all Russian prisoners, some nine thousand of them, were released but immediately armed and sent into action mopping up.

Meanwhile there was a serious shortage of food. Eight Russian prisoners of war had been found starved to death in one of the barracks in their Compound. Added to that our water and electricity had been suddenly cut off; the latter we surmised, because a Russian tank had bulldozed an electric-cable pole on entering the camp! But we were to discover later that they had been cut off at the mains in Lukenwalde. Later that day Russian liaison officers called on the senior Allied Officers in the camp.

In the evening a group of Russian ex-prisoners was ambushed by German civilians and four killed. The civilians were subsequently captured and taken into custody. Firing continued during the night to the North of the camp where the Germans were still resisting. The following day was quiet except for the few occasions when over-flying German aircraft drew spirited bursts of fire from the Russian's anti-aircraft.

At about 6pm that day I went with a detail which comprised another five members of my mess on a meat foraging expedition. We drove in two lorries through Lukenwalde to a small village about 12 km to the southeast. We were expecting to collect it from some butcher's stores, so you can imagine our surprise when we were deposited at a farm and told to fill the two lorries with live cows!

We had to make our way through the village and across some fields to get to the cows. There were bodies of dead soldiers, mostly German, lying all around.

In the gathering dusk, it was a grim sight; the brutal, futile, staring face of warfare. Unbelievably, this was the very first time I had come face to face with the stark horror of war – dead bodies, staring eyes, blood and mud and broken limbs and lives. We, the eagles, had dropped bombs from above, devastated towns and factories, killed, crippled and maimed thousands of men, women and children, but never witnessed the horrors of our own actions. We scurried over the bodies, lying there in the mud, eyes averted. We were in search of live cows. We had to keep alive!

But none of us, with the exception of Vern White, was raised on a farm, and our attempts to round up even one cow were quite farcical. Vern suggested that what we needed was a halter. The Russian captain, who was in charge, was becoming increasingly exasperated and through the interpreter who came along, he managed to get a halter from the reluctant farmer. Before we got it, Al, my pilot, who had been with me throughout our imprisonment, hit one cow on its head with a huge piece of fencing. The cow fell to the ground, stunned, and Al cut its throat with his penknife. Blood spurted everywhere. At the same time the Russian officer let fly a stream of expletives. I did not need to understand Russian to appreciate the poetry. With great difficulty, we managed to drag the dead animal into one of the lorries. Later, with the aid of the halter and making ramps from old planks, we accomplished the somewhat easier, but nonetheless exhausting task of driving eleven live cows into the two awaiting lorries.

The triumphant ride back to the camp was a nightmare. I was trapped by the weight of the shifting bulk of the cows hard against the side of the lorry. The poor beasts, out of sheer panic, relieved themselves loudly and precipitously. I was splattered, for my part in the whole episode, with a bountiful benediction, warm, moist and extremely revolting. By the time we arrived back at the camp, being cheered like conquering heroes, I was feeling utterly filthy and miserable. But not for long. The laughter and back-slapping that greeted us made our ordeal well worth it!

That night another extract from the British Intelligence summary informed us that:

> "About 600 French civilian prisoners of war, including women, arrived during the day from a Stalag in the Lichterfelde suburb of Berlin, where there were also some American and British. They stated that the Russian Forces occupied Lichterfelde on Saturday afternoon, April 12 and told them to walk to Lukenwalde. On the way here Russian tanks, artillery and infantry were seen in large numbers."

During the night there was a slight scare when a German aircraft fired a burst of 20mm cannon at the Norwegian kitchen barracks, where a light had been showing. That night some of the cows were slaughtered and the next day, April 24, the soup contained bits of meat.

I spent the morning cleaning myself up!

Later, the electric supply was reconnected and news reached us that the Russian and the American forces would soon be linking up at Wittenberg on the Elbe. Things were beginning to improve and hope flickered again in our hearts.

April 25, the day of the San Francisco conference, the water situation was still grim, but we decided to make a huge cake while we still had the ingredients. Our hopes continued to rise when we heard that General Ruge, the Senior Allied Officer, had arrived back at the camp during the afternoon. But alas, he had no hard news about any plans for our repatriation. The questions we wanted answered were when and by what route we would be going home. Would it be via Odessa by the Russians, as rumoured, or westwards through the American lines? But there were no answers. In an effort to allay our anxieties we were told of the special benefits that lay in store for us on our return to England.

April 26. Owing to the uncertainty that prevailed concerning our repatriation, it was decided that the best policy would be to keep ourselves as occupied as possible. Sporting activities were hurriedly organised – the RAF officers soccer team took on the Irish Guards and I found myself playing hockey for the first time that year.

Later that day the water supply was restored to the camp. The electric booster pump for raising the pressure to supply the camp had been made inoperative for some time when the wires in the woods had somehow been cut. Repairing them had involved the risk of being picked off by snipers hiding within the woods.

With lots of time on our hands, some of the members of my mess and I visited a chapel built by Russian prisoners. It was a simple, beautiful conversion of part of a barrack block, displaying biblical murals painted on sackcloth. This was in complete contrast to the squalor of their billets and a most impressive demonstration of the spirit of man – challenging the assumption that religion had no place in a Communist State. I recalled the very moving open air service that had commemorated the prisoners who had been shot whilst escaping from Stalag Luft 3. I was moved in the same way by this chapel – a tangible expression of man's spiritual roots, despite man's inhumanity to man. It transcended all political and cultural ideology and bigotry. It was difficult to comprehend that men had died of starvation in that very compound.

The Russians visited us almost daily now. They filmed the funeral of the Russian prisoners who had died. There had been no service; just a few spoken words and a salute by rifle fire. They seemed particularly impressed by the organization, morale and discipline of the British personnel despite the primitive conditions under which we lived. They wanted to see the barracks of the aircrew – the place where the eagles lived!

~ A Member of the RAF of Indeterminate Race ~

During the afternoon, we were visited by one of Koniev's staff, Major General Famin of the Repatriation Board. He informed us that the time and method of our repatriation had not been decided and on being further questioned, said that there was 'no immediate prospect' of an early repatriation, but that it would most likely be to the west, although not ruling out the possibility of going via Odessa. He said that the whole question of repatriation of prisoners was being dealt with through diplomatic channels! He greatly deplored the conditions in which we had to live and said he would be making arrangements to have us moved to better quarters.

But this was the very thing we dreaded most. We could see no point in moving anywhere except back home. We could not understand the delays and made this clear. We brooded on our situation all through the following day, April 27th. We seemed to be caught up in a state of limbo. Even the news of the actual link-up of the Allied forces could not cheer us up.

The following day, April 28, the first members of the Russian Repatriation Committee arrived. The talk centred on arranging entertainments and not on repatriation. We were told that high-ranking officers dealing with repatriations and accompanied by an International commission would shortly be visiting us. It sounded like so much red-tape. The food situation had improved somewhat since the arrival of the Russians, and this was as well, as the number at the camp had risen to thirty thousand. But our main priority was getting home while the only talk was about entertainment; it seemed as if we were destined to be incorporated into a new Russian province.

~ A Member of the RAF of Indeterminate Race ~

Meanwhile gunfire continued throughout the night and the greater part of following day. News that Himmler had offered to surrender to the British and Americans, but not to the Russians came through. The Germans seemed prepared to fight the Russians to the death. They were well aware that the brutality and devastation they had unleashed on Russia would inevitably lead to reciprocal acts of barbarity upon themselves.

29 April: rumours of an impending move to better quarters were becoming rife as fighting continued in the immediate vicinity of the camp. A Russian colonel, paying a visit to the Senior Allied Officer, estimated that there were still approximately 15,000 German soldiers loose within a 16-mile radius of Lukenwalde. They were in disorganised bands, hungry, desperate and trying to drive west. There was always the possibility of being attacked by these men. Gunfire close to the camp continued throughout the day.

On May 1st a shell landed in the camp, but fortunately, no one was hurt. Fires were seen in the direction of the town and during the night the sound of battle became quite loud. Our sentries claimed they could actually hear the voices of the troops! And then the news that Hitler was dead came through. There was no news about how he had met his end. Nothing really surprised us any more. To hell with Hitler! All we wanted to hear was news of when we would be getting out of this crummy hole.

On May 2nd shells were flying over the compound at frequent intervals and several landed inside. The sporadic chatter of machine gun fire kept us on our toes as bullets fizzed overhead. Everywhere the Germans were making their last stand. We were witnessing the final dying gasps as their panzer divisions ground to a halt. By evening the news came that Berlin had fallen, that Hamburg was now an open city and that the Germans had surrendered in northern Italy.

During these last days of the war, our food reserves had been dangerously low. There was lots of flour but little else. We lived on pancakes and 'panzer-brot'; the latter symbolic of the impending German surrender – flattened loaves, as if a panzer division had driven over them. Displaced persons, mostly Italians, streamed into the camp in their hundreds whilst German prisoners passed by outside – S.S infantry and Luftwaffe aircrew. They were in a shocking physical condition, a column of about 5,000 escorted by just two Russians, one at the head of the column and the other bringing up the rear. Yet none of these prisoners seemed willing to contemplate dodging into the surrounding woods.

May 3. Lukenwalde was mentioned on the BBC news as an area where heavy fighting was taking place. In the last few days 120,000 prisoners had been taken. To our great delight, two American war correspondents visited the camp in a 9th Army jeep. They had crossed the Elbe at the Barby bridgehead, south of Schonebeck and through the link-up area at Wittenberg. They had passed right through the Russian lines without passes and had been greeted by German civilians like long-lost brothers. They had witnessed the mass surrender of an entire German Division and Germans trying to swim across the Elbe to the American lines!

May 4. Today we had an official visit from the American forces, the outcome of which was a statement that American, British and Norwegian personnel would be evacuated the following day! A convoy of lorries was on its way! Our excitement was unbounded.

But the pattern of events of the past four months was to repeat itself. The following day, May 5, our hopes were dashed yet again. Only the sick would be moved. The expected lorries were part of an ambulance convoy.

And so it was not surprising that hundreds of prisoners began taking things into their own hands and making off. I was sorely tempted, but Al, my pilot, thought the risk too great. Why take the chance at this late stage after all we'd been through together? But I was definitely uneasy. Later that day, the convoy arrived and twenty-two American ambulances began to move most of the sick that day.

Then hopes were raised again with an announcement that the long-awaited evacuation of all American, British and Norwegians personnel would begin the next day, this time by US Army trucks. There surely could be no mistake this time, we thought.

That evening nineteen American lorries, driven by black American GIs, suddenly arrived at the camp. What a special joy it was for me, personally, to see so many brothers! They were greeted even more enthusiastically than the mixed Mongolian-looking troops who had liberated us two weeks previously. So much had happened in that time.

The following day, May 6, we eagerly queued up to register with the Russians and the evacuation began at 4.30 pm. But after about two thirds of the Americans had been evacuated, the Russians again intervened and suspended operations! There had been some misunderstanding, but no one could offer any explanation of what it had been. We were so exasperated and deflated we could have given up there and then, and I, for one, did not intend to sit around any longer for anyone.

At about 8pm that evening the Russians tried to explain that the authorisation they required had not been forthcoming from their headquarters and as a result we would not be allowed to leave with the Americans. We did not feel that we could comply with this order and unanimously decided that we would ignore it.

But the following day, May 7, as we started boarding the lorries, the Russians fired shots in the air as a warning. This infuriated us. It seemed that the eagles' wings were being unceremoniously clipped! To add insult to injury, the lorries were turned back and would be returning empty. The reason for the strange attitude of the Russians, who had been so helpful up to this point, was only made clear on a Russian broadcast two days later.[13]

But I was only to learn about it much later, for I had already left the camp...

After we had been prevented from leaving, I made up my mind that I would leave at the first possible opportunity.

---

[13] The reason given was the alleged holding by the Allies of 800 Russian officers who had been captured fighting with the Germans in Normandy shortly after D-Day. I have never been able to verify whether any such thing had happened.

Shortly after this came the news that we had always prayed for: *Der Krieg ist fertig!* The WAR IS OVER! The news spread like wildfire through the camp. We were torn between an overwhelming sense of relief and one of deep frustration. A kind of hysteria prevailed. We were smiling but tense. I knew that nothing was going to stop me leaving now.

Situations like these are breeding grounds for rumour. Another started spreading through the camp – that the American lorries were parked some distance away. This time I decided to check it out for myself. I sneaked out of the camp and ran until I came to a place where the lorries were, indeed, waiting. I felt as if they were waiting just for me. I gathered that they were undecided whether they should be returning to base with their trucks empty or continue waiting for orders. But I already knew my course of action. I would have no difficulty passing for a black American and I put it to the drivers that I would like to go along with them when they eventually left. This they were very willing to do, but they could not move without orders from their own headquarters. They confirmed that they would not be leaving in any case until the following day, so they suggested that I return early the following morning when everyone would be asleep. And that was more-or-less how it transpired. It looked as if it was going to be much easier than I could have hoped for.

I went back to camp and told Al what I had in mind and begged him to come along with me next morning. But he thought I was making a mistake. However, he did not try to dissuade me in any way. He wished me luck. I think he was sure that he would get back to England before me. Well, we would see...

I left very early in the morning of May 8, VE Day. It was still dark as I made my way towards the trucks and I was about half way there when I heard footsteps behind me. I stopped apprehensively and waited, crouching low behind some bushes. When the person came abreast I recognized him at once as a South African officer with whom I had never exchanged a word in prison. Here, we were of the same mind and glad to see each other. I told him where I was headed and he asked if he could join me. We decided to team up on this last stage of our adventure.

We came upon the trucks shortly after. The American guard had heard us approaching and roused those nearest him. They were delighted to see us and gave us hot coffee and biscuits. As it became light more defectors from the camp were turning up. As soon as the first truck was loaded, the brother started up the engine and we were on our way. It was as simple as that. They, no doubt, thought that this was an official evacuation and had asked no questions.

The driver started to make for the nearest route across the Elbe. We were quite delirious now, me and my new found South African buddy. White South African attitudes towards the majority black population did not prevent the feeling of camaraderie that prevailed.

That day, I was to be more harried than I had thought possible. When, after what seemed hours, we reached the Elbe, we were stopped by the Russians. There was no interpreter. No one understood us. We were simply sent packing. We were to spend the best part of twelve hours trying to get a permit to cross over to the American lines. We had tried every known crossing point along the Elbe, but the Russians were most uncooperative and always turned us away. At one point they even tried to send us to a Displaced Persons camp.

This had been the pattern of the last few months, the plight of the eagles. Our feelings of dejection and frustration were overpowering. We were also, by now, absolutely shattered, physically, mentally and emotionally. It was getting dark and we knew that a curfew would be in force by 6pm. Then suddenly someone remembered the Barby Bridgehead, where the two American war correspondents who had visited the camp had crossed.

We turned about and headed for it, our hearts racing and hope born again. It became a race against time. With just a few minutes to go to curfew we caught sight of the pontoon bridge in the distance. As we raced towards it, we saw a single Russian sentry at his post guarding it. As we drew closer he shuffled into the centre of the road peering at us. His expression was not unfriendly but our hearts were really thumping. This was our last chance. Would we be stopped again? Behind the sentry lay the pontoon bridge stretching across the Elbe. We could see movement on the other side as some American soldiers casually looked across the bridge in our direction. We kept heading for the bridge. The sentry moved to one side, came to attention and saluted. We drove straight on past him and in a moment were crossing to freedom.

This was a dream, surely. Any moment now I'd awaken and be back in my louse-ridden sack at Lukenwalde. But it was no dream. My ordeal of the last three and a half months was indeed, finally over. Five days later I was back in England having travelled by truck across Germany – via Schonebeck, Magsburg, Braunswick to Hildesheim; then by plane over the Ruhr, where we witnessed for ourselves the devastation our bombs had caused during those fateful bombing raids. We landed at Brussels, where I watched the Belgian victory parade and joined in the celebrations before the final lap by air to an aerodrome near Oxford.

It was cold and wet but nothing could have dampened my spirits, for ahead of me lay the exciting challenge of a brand new life...

Afterword

Al, my pilot, made it two weeks later. The situation at the camp had dragged on for another twelve days. A day in captivity when one is no longer a prisoner seems like a week and a week a lifetime! The Russians apparently had been sorely distressed at the number of defections from the camp, despite having done everything possible to prevent it. Prisoners were discouraged from wandering about in the town and countryside and forced to stay within the camp. Meanwhile, the promised entertainments never materialized and there had been no news about repatriation. The Russians, however, had complained bitterly to the senior officers of the various nationalities, demanding that all personnel remain within the confines of the camp. But despite their efforts some five to six thousand prisoners succeeded in leaving Lukenwalde unofficially.

During this period, a party of about forty officers and NCOs, who had attempted to go west, were brought back by the Russians after first been taken all the way back to Stalag Luft 3, our old Camp at Sagan, which, whilst I was there, had accommodated 12,000 American and British Air Force officers. It now held 143,000 German prisoners and Sagan was now part of Poland! At the Yalta Conference early in 1943 the western leaders, Churchill and Roosevelt, acquiesced to Stalin's demands that the western boundary of Poland be extended to the rivers Oder and Neisse and that the Polish corridor be eliminated, its eastern boundary reverting to the Curzon line.

Being a prisoner of war taught me a lot about myself. It gave me, at a crucial point in my life, time to reflect and look at myself and society. It taught me many lessons. How to live with other people, even when one did not particularly care for them; that there were always individuals that one could respect, like my Canadian pilot Alton Langille, a courageous and cheerful, natural leader, and the Englishman, Flight Lieutenant Charlie Russell, a cultivated and sensitive human being who had been a great inspiration to me.

I also learned to cope with disappointment and adversity, realising that one does not have to cave in when things do not go the way you want them to; that one could always be doing something positive about any situation one found oneself in, even though it did not win any sort of acclaim or recognition from other people.

In the final analysis it made me aware that warfare was indefensible and barbaric even when it appeared that it could be justified. Peace will never be achieved by a morality which justifies the manufacture and trade in arms, nor by shifting moral stances and allegiances based on expediency and the machinations of power. So-called Superpowers are only those capable of waging the most horrendous forms of warfare by assuming for themselves the sole right to the possession of weapons of mass destruction. Hiroshima could never be justified on whatever grounds. How could the 'civilized' West ever explain this away? How could it live with the memory of the Holocaust? Who possesses the right to produce weapons of mass destruction?

Immediately after my return to England I worked as a liaison officer for the Air Ministry and the Colonial Welfare Office, sitting on the bench at Courts Martial around the country or defending West Indian ground crew in cases involving misdemeanours. On leaving the Royal Air Force I studied law at the Middle Temple and qualified as a Barrister at law.

In July 1993, 50 years and one month after I had been shot down and made a prisoner, I attended an Ecological Festival in Gloebok, Poland. Gloebeck is near Jelenia Gora in southwest Poland, near the Sudaten mountains. This region was known as Silesia and part of Germany during the war. Sagan was some 200 kilometres away and it seemed that I had to make a pilgrimage to the spot where I had been incarcerated for two years.

I revisited Sagan, the site of Stalag Luft 3, where I was first imprisoned, but I never located Belaria, just a few kilometres away, the camp for British officers where I spent most of my time.

The area around Jelina is very beautiful mountain country, and I set off, driven by a young Dutchman who I'd met at the Festival and who had volunteered to take me on this trip. The weather was bright and clear, but after a drive of about a couple of hours, the landscape began to change dramatically. Half way to Sagan there was something quite eerie about the drive along mostly deserted roads, through a monotonously flat and wooded landscape. I recalled the outlook we were so accustomed to in the camps.

When at last we arrived at the spot I could not recognize it as the place where I had been held captive for two years. The barrack blocks had all been pulled down, as had the guard boxes and the perimeter fence. The site was slowly being re-claimed by the surrounding woods. The paths between the barrack blocks and the perimeter fence could still be dis-cerned, marking out the ground plan of the camp. On the side facing the main road was a huge monument with a sculpture of a reclining Belsen type figure, adding to the des-olation of the place. Behind was new purpose-built museum, displaying a model of the camp and POW paraphernalia.

At another end of the site were the rusty, overgrown rail-way lines that led to the station where we would have disembarked all those years ago. The eerie atmosphere that I had felt being driven along those lonely roads was much more pronounced now. Dead silence and a sense of desola-tion and abandonment. Not even the sound of a bird. As I wandered about, ghostly memories came to my mind – pris-oners from all the Allied countries of all ranks, the appels, and *goons* (German *gefreiters)* scurrying about with rifles on their backs and surly expressions on their faces, our walks along the perimeter fence. It occurred to me that even if we had been able to get beyond the fence, the monotony of the vast countryside beyond would have been quite disorientat-ing.

I visited a graveyard nearby, where Allied airmen were bur-ied, a plaque in front bearing their names and ranks – no one that I had known – and the open area we had used as a playground. What was frustrating was that I had no idea in which direction lay Belaria, where I had spent most of my imprisonment. I knew that it was only a few kilometres from the main camp, Stalag Luft 3, but although we drove around and asked the pockets of villagers we came across, none were able to shed any light. The German place names had been changed to Polish, but most of the people seemed to speak only German, which my Dutch friend did not understand. It was all very frustrating. Eventually we gave up, but the shadow of war still hung over the landscape as we set out on our return to Jelenia Gore in the beautiful mountainous countryside.

Cy Grant ~ Curriculum Vitae

1919   Born Guyana (then British Guiana, a Crown Colony).

1941   Joined the RAF, commissioned 1943, became navigator of Lancaster bomber.

1943-45   POW in Germany.

[1948   EMPIRE WINDRUSH]

1950   Qualified as a barrister-at- law, Middle Temple; entry into show business (as a means of survival!)

1951   Member of the Lawrence Olivier Festival of Britain Co, London and New York

1954-56   Singer of folk songs, calypso etc, at Esmeralda's Barn.

1956   Co-starred in the film *Sea Wife* and BBCtv drama *A Man from the Sun* (about plight of immigrants finding employment).

1957   Appeared in Granada TV's *Home of the Brave*, a Play of the Week.

1957-60   Appearances on BBC TV TONIGHT – singing folk songs & topical calypsos; the first black face to appear regularly on British Television but labelled a 'calypso singer'

[1958   NOTTING HILL RIOTS]

1958   Starred in Italian film *Calypso!* – the label had stuck!

1961   Starred in *The Encyclopaedist*, a BBCtv play by John Mortimer; 2-hander with Elizabeth Shepherd.

1963   Concert: 'British Week' in Munich – at the Kongress Hall of the Deutschen Museums.

1965   *Othello* – Leicester Repertory

[1966   GUYANESE INDEPENDENCE]

1966   Appeared in *Cindy Ella* – a musical with Cleo Laine and
           Elizabeth Welch – at the Garrick Theatre, London, also
           in a BBCtv Christmas Show, on BBC Radio and recorded
           a LP record.

[1968   Enoch Powell 'Rivers of Blood' speech]

1968   Poetry included in *Black Words* published by Blue Foot
           Traveller, *Caribbean Voices*

1971   Appeared in concert at the Queen Elizabeth Hall

1973   Appeared in the film *Shaft in Africa*

1973   Considered returning to the Bar – Chambers – Middle
           Temple

1974   Appeared in film *At the Earth's Core*

1974   Chairman/co-founder of DRUM Arts Centre, the first
           workshops for black actors, leading to workshops at the
           National Theatre. Drum was set up by Cy Grant and
           John Mapondera in 1974 with the aim of creating a na-
           tional centre for the arts of black people. In June 1975
           Drum organized a two-week season at the Institute of
           Contemporary Arts of plays by West Indian writers,
           combined with an exhibition of carnival photographs
           and costumes, performances by steel bands, etc. as part
           of Mass in the Mall. One of these plays, *Sweet Talk* by
           Michael Abensettes, went on to the Kings Head. In the
           same year Drum also presented two plays at the Com-
           monwealth Institute – *How Do You Clean A Sunflower?*
           and Wole Soyinka's *The Swamp Dwellers*. In 1976 Drum
           organised a three month long theatre workshop at Mor-
           ley College, Lambeth, under the direction of Steve
           Carter of the Negro Ensemble Theatre Company, New
           York. As a result of these workshops, *Bread* by Mustapha
           Matura, was presented at the Young Vic as part of the
           National Theatre summer season. This led to the setting

up of workshops with black actors at the National Theatre for two successive years. In 1977, Ola Rotimi, from
the University of Nigeria directed workshops at Morley
College, leading to the production of his play *The Gods
Are Not To Blame* at the Jackson's Lane Community
Centre and The Greenwich Theatre. Drum also staged
art exhibitions in various galleries in London, the most
impressive (co-ordinated by Irene Staunton) being *Behind the Mask - Afro-Caribbean Poets and Playwrights in
Words and Pictures* at the Commonwealth Institute and
the National Theatre in 1979.

1976   Appeared in *The Ice Man Cometh* with the Royal Shakespeare Co, London.

1977-79   One-man performance in *Return To My Native Land
"Cahier d'un Retour aux pays Natal"* by Aime Cesaire,
a product of the negritude movement. Also at the National Theatre (*Platform Performance*), Theatre
Upstairs, Royal Court Theatre and on tour for two years

[1981   INNER CITY RIOTS]

1982-87   Director of Concord Multicultural Festivals. Between
1981 and 1985 Concord mounted 20 multicultural festivals in major theatrical venues in cities in England and
Wales. These were followed by two county-wide festivals
– in Devon (1986) and Gloucestershire (1987). The aim
of Concord was to celebrate the cultural diversity that is
the reality of life in Britain today, via the authentic arts
of all cultures, particularly unrecognised local arts. The
Festivals included performances by local, national and
international artists, workshops, exhibitions and some
educational residences. A report on Concord in Devon is
available on application. It provides a blue print of good
practice and was largely responsible for the develop-
ment of the multicultural arts policy adopted by the Art
Council.

1989   *Tree of Liberty in the Caribbean* with Jenny Zobel; narrative anthology Bi-centenary French Revolution, Purcell Room, Cheltenham International Literary Festival.

1989   'One Love Africa' Save the Children Fund International Music Festival   Zimbabwe

1989   start writing Blackness and the Dreaming Soul

1993   *Calypso Chronicles* series (6 programmes) for BBC Radio 2

1994   *Panning for Gold* – 2 programmes for BBC Radio 2

1995   *Amazing Grace* – BBC Radio 2

1996   Researching book *Ring of Steel* – visit Trinidad

1997   Honorary Fellowship, University of Roehampton

2000   Book *Ring of Steel – pan sound & symbol*, Macmillan. The transmutation of industrial waste material (steel drums) into the 20th Century's only acoustic/percussion instrument – pure alchemy! Its rapid world-wide appeal and its power to heal. The book. proposes a theory that tries to deal with the metaphysics of pan sound – the dichotomy that exists between the Western tempered scale and the natural harmonics of the laws of physics we find in other world musics.

2001   Member Scientific & Medical Network, an international forum for creating a new world view for the 21st Century – two articles appear on its website www.scimednet.lorg and one in the Summer Review 2005

2002   Acknowledged as a pioneer of Black Theatre; *Blackstage – an oral history of Black British Theatre*, Theatre Museum London.

2004   Paper *Beyond the Jargon: Multiculturalism Redefined* given at the University of Surrey Seminar "Youth Ethnicity and the future of Multiculturalism in Europe". Multiculturalism not the political expedient of an umbrella of peoples co-existing by limited cultural exchange.

2004   *Daylight Come* – BBC Radio 4

2005   *The Wild Blue* – 'The Archive Hour' – BBC Radio 4

2005   Article 'Return to the Source' in *Scientific & Medical Network Review*

2006   Book *Blackness & the Dreaming Soul* published by Shoving Leopard. "As a participatory observer of the dominant Western way of life, Cy Grant brings a fresh perspective and understanding to the tensions inherent in our prevailing ideologies. He recognises the intrinsic limitations of a world view based on duality, alienation, exploitation, greed and materialism, envisaging the common ground of a harmonious philosophy of non-duality and human interconnectedness with nature. His holistic vision is truly multicultural, implying a new era of mutual respect and the end of a Western monopoly on definitions of reality. As such, it is a truly liberating book." [David Lorimer in *Scientific & Medical Network*]

2010   Cy Grant died on 13th February, aged 90; he was survived by his wife Dorith and their four children.

Index